SNAKE CATCHER

TrueStoriesandReptileFacts

SNAKE CATCHER

TrueStoriesandReptileFacts

Tony Harrison & David Blissett

M
MELBOURNE BOOKS

Published by Melbourne Books
Level 9, 100 Collins Street,
Melbourne, VIC 3000
Australia
www.melbournebooks.com.au
info@melbournebooks.com.au

Title: Snake Catcher: True Stories and Reptile Facts
Authors: Tony Harrison and David Blissett
ISBN: 9781922129406 (paperback)

A catalogue record for this
book is available from the
NATIONAL
LIBRARY
OF AUSTRALIA   National Library of Australia

Dedications

Tony: For Bernie and Christine Harrison
— thanks for putting up with a lifetime of critters.

David: For Cathie
— thank you for letting me quit my day job to follow a dream.

And to Dr Harry Butler AO CBE
— for helping two young blokes stand up and take notice.

Contents

Introduction

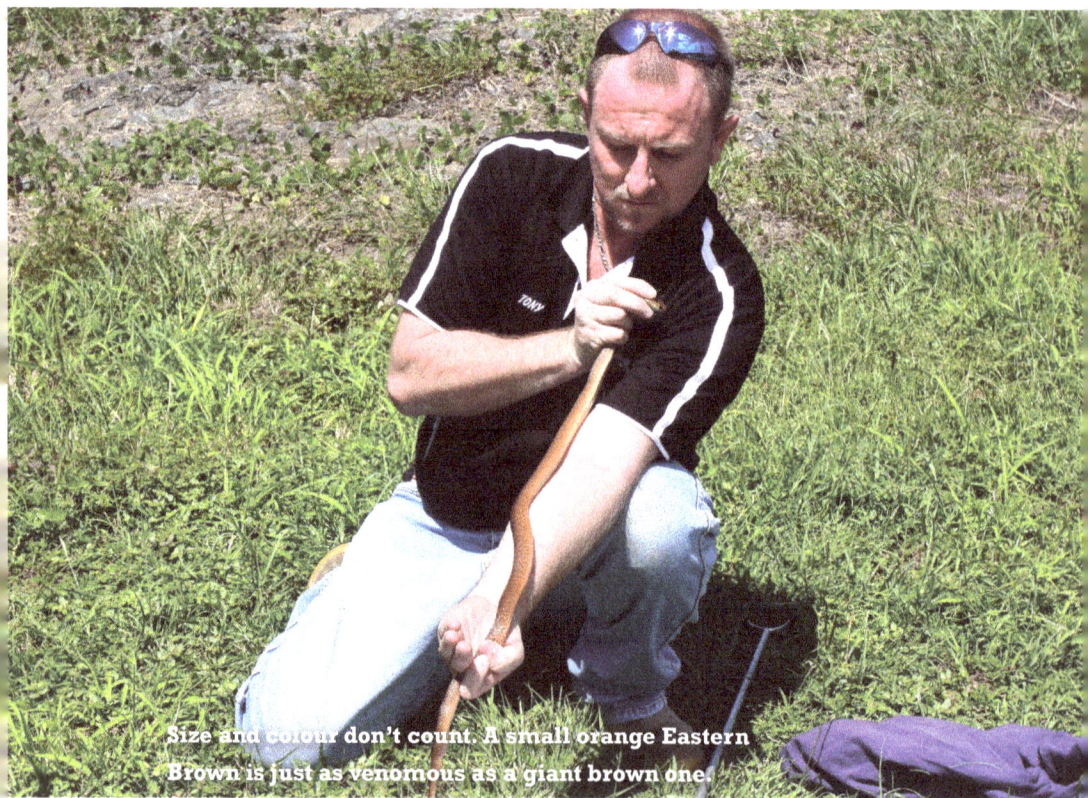

Size and colour don't count. A small orange Eastern Brown is just as venomous as a giant brown one.

In the following pages, you will read stories of Tony Harrison, one of Australia's highest-profile snake catchers. They are all 100% true. Tony has lived the life of a professional snake catcher for almost two decades. He has spent his whole life surrounded by reptiles. That means he has a tale or two to tell. And he also has the pictures to prove it. Most of the photographs you will see throughout this book were taken by Tony himself.

However, more than telling a few good stories and showing some great pictures, this book has another purpose. We want show you some truly fascinating reptiles and provide some common sense advice, from an expert, about living safely with them. We'll introduce some of the reptiles commonly encountered in our cities and towns, including some of the most venomous snakes in the world. We'll tell you what to do, and what not to do.

People are often afraid of reptiles, and snakes hold a particular terror. 'The only good snake is a dead snake' is a mantra. Yet, our increasing encroachment into bushland areas, and the way we often inadvertently encourage them onto our properties, brings us closer to many of these original custodians of the land

Australia is a land of reptiles. We are blessed with some of the most diverse, beautiful, and yes, dangerous reptiles on the planet. We can, however, learn to live with them and, as Tony shows, even benefit from having them around. There are many more species to discover — more than 20 species of snake live on the Gold Coast alone. The fact sheets featured throughout this book provide information and advice on the most commonly-seen reptiles in the more populated areas of Australia.

Please enjoy.

Chapter 1

A Day with Tony

It's October 2013, and it's unseasonably hot. The sky is screaming blue. The land shivers under a punishing sun. It's perfect weather for critters with a hankering for heat. We're in Ormeau, an industrial suburb between Queensland's capital city Brisbane and the world-famous holiday strip of the Gold Coast. We're walking along a fence line, with cargo sheds and shipping containers on one side, an earth bank and a wide bitumen parking area on the other. There's rubbish on the ground, piles of leaf litter accumulated under a handful of small gum trees, and in the middle of it all, there are two of the world's most dangerous snakes, twisted together.

'See those two,' a man's voice says, pointing us in the right direction. 'Eastern Browns mating. Ohhh mate, look at the size of them.'

That's unusual. There are nerves in his voice. I detect genuine concern. He usually doesn't sound this way — not at all. But then I remember: this is the species of snake that came close to killing him a few years back. We're within a few metres of the second most venomous land animal on earth, there are two of them, they're huge — as thick as twisted forearms — and they may well be mating. This isn't likely to go smoothly.

Ordinarily, you'd give a pair of snakes like this a really wide berth. In fact, you should give any snake a wide berth, unless you know what you're doing. That isn't an option for this man. He's been called here to deal with the problem, not step around it. He knows what he's doing, but he still sounds on edge.

He moves forward, and now we can have a better look at him. He's a stout bloke, dressed in a black tee-shirt and jeans, ankle-length walking boots, a long brown goatee, and a pair of shades resting on his shaved head. He walks quickly ahead, right up to the two snakes, stands over them, legs and arms apart, sizing up the task and ready to move when he has to. And move quickly.

He reaches forward — a feint — and then quickly retreats. They've noticed him. Two heads are worse than one. It's a tough situation. He tries another strategy, leaning his body in one direction and waving his hand, while reaching forward with the opposite arm. A coffin-shaped brown head strikes out. The man pulls back his arm. The snake misses. He tries again, but it's the same result. A strike and a miss. It's time to rethink the approach.

'When there's love in the air,' the bloke says, 'these things don't give a damn.'

He's right. The two long, thick serpents remained curled together, taut and twisted and refusing to retreat, as almost every snake does when confronted by a human being. Not these two. They're totally absorbed in each other.

As the man moves in again, we can see a crowd is gathering, albeit at a safe distance. Plenty of people work around here. There's a lot of heavy machinery, warehouses and cartons and containers. A million places for a snake to hide. These two need to be caught and removed, to prevent a potential tragedy.

Then, somewhat unexpectedly, the man senses his chance. He throws himself forward, falling onto hands and knees, right into the curl of mating snakes. There's chaos. Snake bodies fly. Leaves scatter. We hear grunting sounds. And then, for what feels like too long, there is silence. All we can hear is the distant wash of traffic and the hum of refrigerated shipping containers. Has our mate been struck? How long does a man have to get medical help, when a snake with this kind of venom has bitten him? And just what is the first aid for snake bite?

Thankfully, he appears again, now holding a very long and very upset snake by the tip of the tail. He has the Eastern Brown Snake out on the end of an extended arm, letting its head and neck touch the ground, but it's a massive animal. The reptile turns on itself and strikes towards the man's groin — and the very thought of being bitten there boggles the mind — but the man anticipates the move and manages to twist the snake away.

'The female disappeared over there,' he says to the assembled crowd, pointing in the direction of the shipping containers and sending a few blokes onto the tips of their toes. 'It's OK, I'll bag this bloke up first. She'll be back in a second. She'll head back to where the mating was taking place. They always do. Dirty little things.'

And then, as he holds the male Eastern Brown in one hand and a long blue catch bag in the other, his mobile phone begins to ring. He coaxes the snake into the bag, reaches into his pocket with a semi-free hand, and takes the phone call.

'Good afternoon,' he says. 'Tony Harrison speaking...'

Fact Sheet

Bandy Bandy

An attractive and intriguing little snake, little is known about the Bandy Bandy, but they do sometimes arrive in people's backyards.

Identification: They are marked unlike any other species of snake. Bandy Bandy's have over 40 high-contrast black and white rings all over their bodies, including their bellies. They have narrow heads and small eyes and grow to about 75 cm in length.

Diet: Feed almost exclusively on the Blind Snake. While venomous, very little is known of the venom strength, however it is not considered dangerous, even though significant reactions have been recorded.

Where found: Northern and Eastern Australia, including areas around Sydney and Brisbane. Common but rarely seen due to behaviour.

Tony says: This is a cool snake. They are pretty little things, with those vivid black and white stripes. They primarily live underground and I generally only get calls for them after heavy rain forces them out of the sodden soil. These guys have a fantastic defence mechanism. Rather than striking, they lift up part of their bodies into a loop shape. And if they get really annoyed, sometimes you get two loops. I reckon that's fair warning to leave him alone.

Bandy Bandy

Bandy Bandy

Fact Sheet

Crowned Snakes

Crowned snakes are reasonably common, but nocturnal. This means people seldom see them, unless there is some sort of feline intervention.

Identification: The Golden-crowned Snake is usually a shade of brown, with red underside and yellow or gold crown markings around the head. The White-crowned is usually grey to dark grey with the crown more cream or white in colour. Both species grow to around 50-75cm. The Dwarf-crowned Snake (not pictured) is similar to his cousins, but only grows to about 25cm and has distinctive v-shaped yellow belly scales.

Diet: All these snakes are lizard eaters, hunting at night to catch lizards as they sleep. They are venomous, but not dangerously so.

Where found: The Golden and Dwarf-crowned Snakes range from north of Sydney to South East Queensland, and the White-crowned is found from Northern NSW to the Whitsundays in Queensland. All species can be found in Brisbane and the Golden-crowned in Sydney. They prefer cooler areas, such as rainforest of the Gold Coast Hinterland or sandstone areas north of Sydney.

Tony says: The most common occurrence with these guys is when your friendly neighbourhood pussy cat is left outside at night, catches one of these snakes and brings it into the house to present to its owners. Crowned snakes are all too happy to puff themselves up, like a cobra and have a strike, especially if they've been chewed on by a cat. It's almost always bluff. They very seldom open their mouth to bite, but people get a shock when they see this display and try to kill the snake. Again, the message is two-fold. First, don't leave your cats to wander at night and second, if you do find one of these guys in your house, don't try to deal with it yourself, but call an expert to help.

Golden-crowned Snake

White-crowned Snake

Chapter 2

Starting Out — in the Boot-steps of Heroes

After all these years, Tony is still the Lizard Kid.

Growing up, most kids have heroes or heroines. They might be superheroes, sporting legends, movie stars, even a favourite relative ... but a television naturalist? I mean, really?

Now imagine the scene: it's sometime in the late 1970s, early evening, and though they are separated by about ten kilometres of grey sandstone ridges and cool green creek-lined gullies, two wide-eyed boys sit down in front of the TV — grass stains on their knees, a grazed elbow or two — while the dial is switched over to the ABC. Their favourite show is about to start.

The two boys are waiting for a grizzled, bearded naturalist in khaki shorts and a bush hat to once again traipse around the Australian outback, unlocking the secrets of this country's wild places in a way no one had done before. This is no voice-over guy. Harry's hands on. He turns over rocks and reaches into hollow logs to see what might be living inside. He is bitten occasionally. Bitten, or scratched. He even bleeds once in a while. And he regularly tells us to get out there and take a look at nature, to enjoy what we find, but to then make sure we put everything back where we found it. His is a message of coexistence with wildlife. Long before Steve Irwin, there was a naturalist, author, TV host and kid's hero, by the name of William Henry 'Harry' Butler.

Harry Butler inspired a whole generation of kids to tramp out to their backyard, or into the nearest bush reserve, start turning over rocks and discover wildlife for themselves. Because of Harry, Australian wildlife suddenly meant more than kookaburras, kangaroos and koalas. His television series, *In the Wild*, showed us there was another world to explore. This was a world of creatures with fins and feathers, exoskeletons and scales. It was a world where the inhabitants had two legs, or eight, or six, and some had none at all. And not everything was cute like a koala, which made the bush seem like a much more stimulating place to be. Harry introduced wildlife to TV audiences in a new and exciting way. It was real. It was raw. His show captured the imagination of millions of people, including two boys living on Sydney's north-western outskirts. I was one of those wide-eyed lads. The other was Tony Harrison.

It was Harry Butler who set me on a dream career path. I wanted to be a park ranger, or a zoo keeper. I wanted to work with animals in some way. Tony Harrison was the same. The boy they called 'Tony the Lizard Kid' wanted to be a naturalist, like Harry was. He would spend hours out in the garden turning over rocks to find 'critters.' We both used to keep reptiles in our bedrooms.

However, as is the way of these things, the dreams of boys are not always straightforward — because if they were, the world would be overrun by police officers, fire fighters or fighter pilots — not every lizard kid grows up to be a zoo keeper or a naturalist. I left school and went into law enforcement. Tony, who was by this time already tinkering in the rapidly expanding world of computers, went into the IT industry.

My government career lasted fourteen years, before I diversified. I tried adult education, community services and, finally, became a professional writer. Still, the dream of being around animals never really left me. I married, moved into a little house on the edge of the bush — not all that far from where I began — and sat back to enjoy the Swamp Wallabies and Ringtail

Possums, the Lyrebirds and Scrub Turkeys, the Diamond Pythons and Red-belly Black Snakes. I started to write their stories, and those of the people who lived with them. And it was through this work that I discovered the website and YouTube channel of the Gold Coast Snake Catcher. A bloke called Tony Harrison. His work fascinated me. I sent him an email. Made a phone call. We agreed to write a book together.

Unlike me, Tony Harrison's wildlife career dreams did come true. The Lizard Kid's time in IT didn't last. Nor did he stay in Sydney. He went north, to start again. The first thing I want to know is why Tony moved away from home in Sydney and how this led him to working full-time with reptiles.

~ ~ ~

'It was kind of by accident,' is how Tony describes the start of things. He worked for eight years in IT before that little voice inside his head became too loud to ignore. You might be familiar with the little voice. It's the one that tells you to sell up, take a punt and do something else with your life. Set up that small business. Buy that holiday house. Drive a red sports car. Live your dreams. Go fishing. Write the great Australian novel.

It was Tony's passion for reptiles which finally necessitated his move north, to the Gold Coast of Queensland.

It's only been in recent years that captive-bred reptiles have been able to be legally kept by private individuals in New South Wales. Back in the 1980s licensing conditions in the state were strict and prohibitive. Tony decided to move to Queensland, where state laws allowed the keeping of captive-bred reptiles as pets. He can't have known it at the time, but it was a decision that would completely change his life.

To pay the bills, and rather than returning to IT, Tony planned to start a fishing charter business on the Gold Coast. By 1992, his business was operating and beginning to attract customers. As the money rolled in, his personal pet collection started to grow as well. I ask Tony if he can remember the first snake he owned after his move to the Coast.

He can. She was a tiny hatchling Coastal Carpet Python called Monty.

'The guy who owned her couldn't get her to feed,' he says. 'So I bought her off him. He was a bloke in my suburb. I still remember he delivered her to me in a packet of smokes.'

It wasn't long until Tony's collection grew. He started earning a reputation as the snake guru of the neighbourhood. And, as is the way of these things, the neighbourhood soon came calling.

'This night, one of my neighbours came running down the street,' Tony remembers. 'She was screaming about the monster snake in her yard.'

He raced up to his neighbour's place, only to find that someone else had 'sorted' the problem. To his distress, Tony found a beautiful, and non-venomous, Carpet Python lying dead. The snake had been mutilated; chopped into pieces. Not only was the act wrong — it's against the law to harm or kill protected wildlife in all States and territories of Australia, except under very specific conditions, such as the protection of human life — but it also reinforced the stereotype that exists among many people in Australia: 'the only good snake is a dead one.'

This single act, and the attitude of those involved, was enough to spur Tony to action. He asked his neighbour why she hadn't called a snake catcher to deal with the python.

'Because,' she replied, 'there aren't any.'

That was when the little voice called out again. Tony saw an opportunity. He decided he'd spread word around the neighbourhood; tell people he was available to capture and relocate any snakes that they found around their homes. His initial motivation was nothing more than saving the lives of a few animals in the local area. It soon proved to be much more than that. His business idea filled a void. And good news travels fast.

By 1994, Tony Harrison was a fully-licensed snake catcher on the Gold Coast. He decided to swap the fishing business for a small snake catching one, or as he puts it, 'I swapped the wet scales for some dry ones.' He began charging clients a small call-out fee to come out, catch, and relocate their snakes. Then, during the cooler winter months, when snake activity ceased, he started working on ways to educate the public about the truth of these complex and magnificently-designed creatures.

Reptile Relocation and Awareness was born.

The calls kept coming. The business grew. Now, in the warmer months between September and May, Tony can receive callouts at any time of the day or night. He often works seven day weeks and 20 hour days. Since he set up the business, Tony has made over 13,000 individual snake calls, across the Gold Coast and South-east Queensland. He receives calls and emails from around Australia and the world. His YouTube channel receives hundreds of thousands of hits every year. In the quieter months, Tony travels to schools, community events, shows and expos, giving reptile talks and snake demonstrations. And his personal collection of reptiles has grown and diversified.

Tony keeps and breeds a wide range of beautiful animals, from the world's smallest pythons to the most venomous land animal alive. He's kept skinks and geckos, monitors and dragons, even the occasional Saltwater Crocodile.

Tony has been on the news and on TV documentary shows, talking about his work and reptiles in general. He has done radio segments. Local print media regularly feature his work in articles. He has made and posted over 1000 YouTube videos.

And even if you've not seen his face, chances are you've seen one of his 'critters'. Tony regularly supplies reptiles for television and movie work. If you've seen the movie *Nim's Island*, watched *Terra Nova*, *Sea Patrol* or *Reef Doctors*, you've probably seen one of Tony's animals. I remember feeling more than a little jealous when I saw one of his pet Lace Monitors make eyes at Lisa McCune! His animals have also appeared in calendars, magazines, music videos, fashion shoots and other 'reptile-worthy' events.

With a passion for photography, Tony has a huge collection of reptile images. You will find some of his best images in these pages.

Yet no matter what type of work he does, Tony's message remains the same. It's the message he learnt from his hero all those years ago. It is the reason for this book. He wants to educate people about reptiles, especially snakes, to help them understand that these are not soulless monsters, but a beautiful and essential part of a healthy ecosystem. He wants to share his passion for reptiles and hope that some of it rubs off on those who listen, or watch, or read. He wants humans to coexist with reptiles, by helping people to see the benefits of living in harmony with the animals around them.

His advice can give people strategies to help reduce the risk associated with having reptiles in and around their homes. Most importantly, Tony's goal is to reduce the number of deaths from reptile-related incidents — both for humans and reptiles — down to virtually zero.

Fact Sheet

Copperhead

A medium-sized venomous snake, which would prefer to be left alone to go looking for its next froggy meal.

Identification: Several species, including the Pygmy, Lowland and Highland Copperhead. Grow to a maximum of 1.5 metres with a medium build. Colour varies, from copper-brown to gold, grey to black. May have cream or while markings around the mouth and sides.

Diet: Primarily a frog eater, but will also eat other snakes and can even be cannibalistic. They are venomous and potentially fatal if a bite is left untreated.

Where found: Southern NSW, Victoria, South Australia and even Tasmania. Commonly found around Melbourne and along the Great Dividing Range where conditions are cooler.

Tony says: This snake is much happier in cooler weather than many species. In fact, when it's too hot, they tend to hunt at night rather than during the day. They like hanging around water, where frogs and other reptiles might be located. I have kept this species for years and found them to be quite shy. They would much prefer to be left alone. If, however, you find one in your backyard or around the house, call your local snake catcher or wildlife authority for assistance.

Copperhead

Copperhead

Chapter 3

Python — The Welcome Visitor

The most commonly seen snakes are the Carpet family of pythons.

Australia is a growing nation. According to the Bureau of Statistics[1], our population has risen from just under 15 million to over 23 million people in the past 30 years. As this expansion has continued, larger tracts of natural bush have been cleared to make room for human activities. Human beings and wildlife have come more and more into contact with each other. The results have been well documented. Hundreds of native species are now rare or vulnerable to extinction. Many species are, in fact, extinct. Lost forever. But then, there are a select few, a handful of creatures, including a number of reptiles, which have found human beings to be ideal life companions. In this chapter we will meet some of them.

~ ~ ~

At our home in Sydney, my wife and I share space with a wide range of native animals, including reptiles. There are Diamond Pythons living in our roof, and they are doing a much better job of rat control than any human-devised methods we've ever tried. We have frog ponds around the yard and receive regular visits, not just from the frogs, but from the frog-eating specialists, such as Red-belly Black and Green Tree Snakes. We have geckos and a range of skink species doing the job on our garden insects, snails and slugs. These creatures are welcomed. We coexist. Regrettably, this is not always the case.

With over 13,000 reptile callouts to his name, Tony Harrison understands better than most, the kinds of things people do to attract reptiles to their homes, often without realising it. I ask him about the most common things he sees in his work.

~ ~ ~

The snakes most commonly encountered by people along Australia's east coast are the Carpet family of pythons (the *Morelia spilota* species). This includes the Coastal Carpet Python, found in Northern NSW and throughout Queensland, and the Diamond Python, found from Central NSW and down into Victoria. In far North Queensland, the Amethystine or Scrub Python (*Morelia amethistina*) — Australia's largest snake — is often found living in and around suburban homes and on farmland.

It's springtime on the Gold Coast and love is in the air. Tony Harrison, however, is not really feeling it. He's up inside a customer's roof. And it's hot. Outside we can hear the sounds of farm animals.

'As you can hear, this place is like Old MacDonald's farm,' Tony says. 'They've got chooks and ducks and geese and sheep and alpacas. Anyway, the lady here has heard sounds up in her roof and wanted me to check it out.'

It wasn't easy for Tony to get into the roof cavity.

'The manhole cover weighed a ton,' he says. 'It had a couple of Carpet Pythons lying on top of it.'

He starts to look around the roof cavity. A rooster crows outside.

'There's one,' Tony says, his torch lighting up the familiar patterned skin of a Carpet Python. He catches and bags the animal. Outside a sheep starts bleating.

'Trouble is ... this roof space is very hot now. The snakes come in here at night and as it gets hotter, they vanish down into the wall cavities where it is cooler. All the farm animals outside have attracted lots of food for snakes and, as you can see, they are up here having a great old time.'

True enough — the topside of the ceiling plaster is festooned in snake droppings. There are shed skins hanging off roof timbers. A rooster crows outside.

'It's likely one of the big snakes up here is a female,' Tony says. 'It's mating season, there's plenty of tucker outside ... it's the bistro ... and then the Carpets are coming up here at night for some good times. This is like a Carpet night club.'

Tony finds five Carpet Pythons in the customer's roof. He can't catch them all — snakes can fit into spaces that humans just can't — but it illustrates a common situation facing people living in areas like the Gold Coast.

These pythons are non-venomous. They hunt, often at night, using camouflage and stealth to track their prey. They have a line of visible heat-sensing pits along their bottom jaws which allow them to detect minute variations in temperature, including the body heat of a mammal or bird. Prey animals are caught using a lightning strike, before being constricted to death by the crushing body coils of the snake.

Tony sees pythons daily during the warmer months. In suitable habitats, as many as one in three homes will have one of these snakes living in or around them. This includes major suburban areas. Tony has even caught Carpet Pythons in the high rise buildings along the Surfers Paradise tourist strip. They are expert climbers and are commonly found in trees, or the roof space of houses.

These pythons will eat anything with fur or feathers. Younger snakes target small birds, mice and sometimes lizards. Adult pythons hunt the larger birds — such as parrots — as well as rats, possums and even fruit bats. Amethystine Pythons, from Far North Queensland, can grow to well over five metres long, large enough to capture and swallow prey the size of a wallaby.

Human activities, including the animals we keep as pets, make our homes more attractive to these stealthy hunters. Our pet foods and our garbage attract rats, which often make nests in our roof spaces. The pythons get to know this and they follow the rodents onto our properties. We feed native wildlife, like birds and possums, which then attract pythons. And sometimes, even our pets can fall victim. Tony has seen it plenty of times.

'Chooks, ducks, birds, guinea pigs,' he says, 'the occasional small dog, and especially cats. About once a month I find a cat that's been taken by a big Carpet Python, usually after dark.'

In the python world, things get busy as soon as winter ends. In early spring, males start to become active. They begin looking for females, and this is often when they come into closer contact with people. Tony starts dealing with roving male Carpet Pythons as early as August.

'This is their one chance of the year to mate,' he explains, 'so they get into all sorts of places where a female might be hiding out, and that includes people's gardens and roof spaces.'

Occasionally a python will find its way inside a home, and this is when problems can occur. Panic sets in. People make errors of judgement. There are injuries, both to snake and human. If you give a python some space, and then give it an avenue of escape, it will often do so in its own time. However, if home owners are worried, they should contact their local wildlife authority or snake catcher. Never try to harm or kill a python. Not only is it illegal, but they have a mouthful of very sharp teeth — '160 to be exact,' Tony reminds me — and they can use those teeth to good effect if they feel threatened.

In reality, people have nothing to fear from these beautiful snakes. And actually, a python can be a beneficial house guest, rather than something to destroy. There are some basic rules Tony recommends to reduce the chances of a python causing dramas.

'Keep your pets indoors, especially cats at night,' is his advice. 'Also, don't leave garbage or food scraps lying around for rats and mice.' But if you do find yourself host to a python, Tony has this to say; 'look, these pythons really are inoffensive fellows. If you don't harass or try to harm them, they will rarely cause you a drama, and in fact they will do you a favour by knocking out your rodent problems.'

Rats and mice can carry disease. They chew electrical cables and timber work. They have been known to cause house fires. Poisons and traps can create more problems than they solve — and if you've ever had to dispose of a putrid rat carcass, you'll understand what we mean. So what better rodent solution than a clean, quiet and harmless resident who will do the job more efficiently than you could ever do, and will charge you nothing for the privilege? For the majority of the time, you won't even know they're around.

There's one more benefit to having a python as a visitor:

'What people also need to realise is these guys are doing you another favour,' says Tony. 'By knocking out your rodents, they are also taking away a food source from another regular, and far more dangerous, snake visitor to many suburban backyards — the Eastern Brown snake.'

We'll meet him next.

Fact Sheet

Carpet Python Family

The snakes most commonly encountered by people on the east coast belong to the Carpet group of pythons. All of these snakes are non-venomous, killing their prey by constriction.

The Coastal Carpet Python

Identification: Between 2 and 4 metres. They vary enormously in colour, with cream, olive, black and brown markings, resembling an oriental carpet. The northern sub-species (see image), sometimes called the 'Jungle Carpet Python' can be a striking gold and black in colour.

Diet: Anything with fur or feathers, including rodents, birds, possums and even fruit bats.

Where found: From Northern NSW to Central and North Queensland. Very common. There are various sub-species/forms of the Carpet Python, found across Central, Southern and Western Australia. This includes the Diamond Python (see below).

Tony says: I find these guys more than any other snake type. Statistically one in three homes in SE Queensland has a Carpet Python living in or around it.

Coastal Carpet Python

Jungle Carpet Python

The Diamond Python

Identification: Similar in size to Carpet Python, but darker body colour, with yellow and white markings, usually in diamond patterns.

Diet: As per Carpet Python.

Where found: Found from Central NSW to Victoria. Commonly found around Sydney

Tony says: This snake is very closely related to the Coastal Carpet and the two can inter-breed. In areas where their ranges overlap — such as the mid-north coast of NSW, we see snakes with characteristics of both types. Diamonds are common in the bushland suburbs of Sydney, including the Blue Mountains.

Carpet and Diamond Pythons do home owners a big favour. They eat the rats and mice that would otherwise attract venomous snakes like Eastern Browns. However sometimes I find them with household pets in their bellies, including cats. If you have outdoor pets in hutches — such as rabbits or guinea pigs — make sure their cages have strong, narrow mesh, to keep snakes out. Cats should be kept indoors, especially at night, when they are most likely to be attacked. My recommendation if you see these guys around is to leave them alone. They aren't venomous, but with over 150 teeth, they still pack a nasty bite. If a python is inside your home, or if you are concerned, call a snake catcher or local wildlife authority.

Diamond Python

Fact Sheet

The Amethystine (Scrub) Python

This is the longest snake in Australia. Another python, these guys are not venomous, but do have hundreds of needle sharp teeth, and a reputation as biters.

Identification: Australia's longest snake. Can grow in excess of 5 metres. They are slender-bodied with brown and cream markings, and an amethyst-like sheen to their scales.

Diet: Mammals and birds. Larger specimens can eat prey the size of a wallaby. Have been known to take family pets, including dogs and cats.

Where found: North Queensland, often seen by residents living in and around Cairns.

Tony says: These guys have a bit of a reputation as aggressive. Even my pet Scrubby, 'Alice' is a handful. It sometimes feels safer working with venomous snake than handling her. As the suburbs of cities like Cairns continue to encroach on the natural world, we are seeing more examples of these big guys coming into contact with people. If you see one while you are out walking in the rainforest, leave them alone and they will go about their business without any problems. If you have one living in or around your home, there are a number of snake catchers operating in the north who will be able to help you out.

Scrub Python

Chapter 4

Red Alert: The Lethal Eastern Brown

Common and potentially a life taker - the Eastern Brown Snake.

Australia's east is home to the second most venomous land snake on earth, the Eastern or Common Brown Snake *(Pseudonaja textilis)*. With super toxic venom, incredible speed and a flighty nature, Tony believes this is the most dangerous snake in Australia. Perhaps the world. And ironically, humans are doing everything right so far as this species is concerned. He sees them very regularly in his job.

'There are two things Eastern Browns love,' Tony says, 'concrete slabs for shelter and lots of rats and mice for a feed.'

Our homes, often built on concrete slabs, and the rodents we attract, mean that the Eastern Brown feels right at home living close to humans. They have a fast metabolism, are big eaters, and they have come to learn that humans provide a ready supply of rodents, without having to search too hard to find them. We moved into their neighbourhood. They decided to stick around.

The name 'Brown' Snake can be a little misleading. Though many Eastern Browns are in fact dull brown in colour, they can be chocolate, cream, grey, striped, spotted, even orange or jet black. The most definitive way to identify this species is that they all have orange or ochre coloured spots on the underside of their belly.

Though, according to Tony; 'if you are close enough to see the orange belly spots of an Eastern Brown, it's probably the last thing you will see before the red and blue lights arrive to take you to hospital.'

What makes the Eastern Brown Snake so dangerous is not just

its venom toxicity, but the speed at which it delivers a strike. These snakes are short-tempered and fast. No, fast doesn't describe it ... they are off the dial so far as speed is concerned.

'An Eastern Brown can strike six times in a single second,' Tony tells me.

Think about that for a moment: six times in one ... single ... second. It's faster than most people can blink. And while they won't chase a person for no reason, if they feel cornered or under threat, Eastern Brown Snakes have been known to defensively strike out and challenge an intruder.

However, there are ways people can protect themselves against these dangerous snakes. First, remove any unwanted building materials or rubbish from your yard. These provide great hiding spots for snakes like Eastern Browns. Keeping lawns mowed and gardens under control can also deter these snakes. Importantly, clean up after pets and don't leave food such as bird seed or cat and dog bowls out to attract rodents, since these rodents will then attract snakes.

There is another important fact to consider. Eastern Browns belong to a group of snakes called elapid, or front-fanged snakes. The fangs act a little like hypodermic needles, piercing the skin and allowing venom to run down into the tissue of anything they bite. Eastern Brown venom is incredibly toxic. However, the fangs in this particular species are very very short. Tony has a great tip.

'If you're out in the bush, or in places where these guys are likely to be,' he says, 'wear good heavy shoes, thick socks and long pants, like jeans. If you are doing the garden, wear thick gardening gloves. Their fangs are tiny little things, so these simple measures will protect you from most bites of this snake.'

Most importantly, if you do see a snake that you think might be an Eastern Brown, do not try to harass or kill it. If you are out in the bush, leave it alone or, if it is in or around your home, call your local snake catcher or your wildlife authority for assistance.

~ ~ ~

It's early spring, 2013. Tony is on a rural property, belonging to a lady who breeds horses. This is perfect snake country, surrounded by open woodland with plenty of stock feed to attract rats and mice. There are stables and animal pens set on concrete slabs, which provide the perfect homes for snakes such as Eastern Browns. Indeed, the customer has seen an Eastern Brown in recent days.

Tony explains to the lady that he can — and will — be able to remove the Eastern Brown, but the characteristics of her property, which made it so attractive to this snake in the first place, will almost certainly attract others. Eastern Browns have such potent venom, that if they bite an animal as big as a horse, and if their fangs are able to penetrate the skin, the horse is likely to die.

'This lady had the full package,' Tony explains. 'Those concrete slabs under her stables are like a five star hotel to an Eastern Brown. And with all the stock feed around, the rats and mice provide a smorgasbord. But I explained to her that we might look at a mixed solution. I can remove the current Eastern Brown she has, but to help prevent others from coming in, I suggested that we might release a few Carpet Pythons to tackle her rodent issues. An Eastern Brown can kill a horse, a Carpet Python — no matter how big — is harmless to such a big animal. And 'hey presto', the customer agreed.'

Tony releases five Carpet Pythons — caught on other customers' properties, earlier in the day — onto the lady's land. It's a great result for Tony. It's heartening to see people working with nature, rather than trying to fight against it.

Fact Sheet

Eastern (Common) Brown Snake

This high venomous snake feels right at home in company with humans. It is very common across the eastern half of Australia.

Identification: Can grow up to a length of 2 metres. Though most often brown in colour, this species can be grey, black, even shades of red. They may have stripes, spots or speckles. Underside of the body is cream, with ochre coloured spots or blotches.

Diet: Primarily a rodent eater, but occasionally also eat lizards or frogs. Has a high metabolism and is a voracious feeder. Highly venomous and potentially lethal.

Where found: Common along the eastern half of Australia, including Sydney, Melbourne, Brisbane and Adelaide. For people living in Perth and Southern WA, the Dugite is a commonly seen relative of the Eastern Brown Snake.

Tony says: In my opinion, this is the most dangerous snake in Australia — and maybe the world. They have the second most toxic venom of any land snake on the planet and they adapt well to built-up areas. They are also flighty and prone to defend themselves if they feel threatened. However, they have very very small fangs. So, if you are in snake country, bushwalking or out in the garden, wear well-built covered shoes, thick socks and long pants like jeans. If you see a snake that you think might be an Eastern Brown, leave it alone. Move slowly and stay a few metres away. If it is on your property and you are concerned, call a snake catcher or your local wildlife authority. The vast majority of bites from this guy are a result of people trying to catch or kill them. Don't take the risk. It's against the law. It could get you killed.

Eastern Brown Snake

Chapter 5

The Green and The Red

Snake colour is misleading - a black Green Tree Snake.

The Green or Common Tree snake *(Dendrelaphis punctulata)* is another species Tony regularly encounters.

Tony Harrison is standing in the middle of a girl's bedroom. It's not his girl's bedroom, it's a customer.

'This is a girl who could grow up with a fear of snakes,' Tony says.

There's nothing especially unusual about the bedroom — mess on the floor, soft toys scattered around the place, boy band posters on the wall — the girl's bed is in a riot.

Tony reaches down to the bed and gently pulls back the floral quilt and the unmistakable shape of a snake begins to move.

'The poor girl felt it moving on her during the night. You can imagine what sort of panic set in.'

He picks up the snake. It's a Green, or Common, Tree Snake; olive green on top, yellow below; whip thin and just over a metre long. It begins to wiggle and thrash in Tony's fingers, but can't get away.

'Now these guys are totally harmless,' Tony tells the girl's parents. 'The worst thing about them is the stink they give on when you hold them. But you wouldn't be able to tell what kind of snake it is in the dark. And in any case, these guys can come in a whole range of colours. They are tree snakes, so they can climb really well. Probably a good idea to check your beds before you turn out the lights from now on.'

'How could it get inside?' the mother asks as Tony takes the snake outside to put in a catch bag.

'Snakes can fit into a space that's one third their girth. And this is a pretty thin snake to begin with, so it doesn't need much room to be able to squeeze inside. They often enter houses through gaps in garage doors.'

Tony bends down near the closed garage door, and right on cue, the snake begins to worm itself in through the gap.

'See,' Tony says. 'Easy as that.'

These Common Trees Snakes are rear-fanged, or colubrid, snakes, and are found right along the Australian east coast, as far south as East Gippsland in Victoria. As is the case with the Brown Snake, the name 'Green' can often be a misnomer. Tony has seen these long slender tree climbers in black, grey or blue, even brown and golden-red.

'I've also heard a lot of people call them 'Yellow-bellied Black Snakes', Tony tells me, 'but there is no such species and these guys are not related in any way to the Black Snake family.'

Comfortable both in trees and on the ground, Common Tree Snakes hunt frogs and small lizards. They are not venomous. Tony often finds them in and around homes with water features. Being a slender-bodied animal, these snakes sometimes find their way into houses. Tony has found this species in garages, in electrical boxes, on staircases, hiding in lounge rooms, in high rise buildings, even inside people's beds. And when these things happen, the trouble can start.

'People see a snake, especially one that looks dark, black or brown, and they immediately think it's something dangerous, and so they try to kill it.' Tony has two problems with people taking this kind of action. 'One, they might kill a perfectly harmless and protected snake, or two, they might actually be taking on something really dangerous and earn themselves a trip to hospital.'

Common Tree Snakes are inoffensive and harmless. They are runners, not fighters. If you give them room to escape, they will almost always take that option. However, if cornered or attacked, they will puff themselves up and strike in self-defence. They also emit a pungent odour when threatened, which Tony reckons is far worse than being bitten by one. I'll take his word on that.

~ ~ ~

If you ask an Australian for their idea of a dangerous snake, they will most likely give you a description of a Red-bellied Black (*Pseudechis porphyriacus)*. It kind of makes sense. Red-bellies do look like they mean business, with their shining black bodies, eyes like onyx marbles, and their blood-red side and belly scales. Yet, if ever a snake had an undeserved reputation, it's this species.

'Red-bellies are really a placid snake,' Tony explains. 'They tend to retreat rather than show any defensive behaviour. However, if they are threatened, they will flatten out their neck, a bit like a cobra and, if really provoked, they will strike.'

The toxicity of Red-belly venom has also been overstated, according to Tony. 'There have been very few deaths from the bite of this species. And although the venom can cause intense pain and other complications — which do require medical attention — generally only people with weak hearts or compromised health are at serious risk of death.'

When Tony started snake catching in the nineties, Red-bellied Black Snakes were in decline in South-east Queensland. He would rarely catch one. There was a simple, if unpleasant explanation.

'When I started snake catching, the Cane Toad was really making its presence felt in this part of Queensland,' Tony says. 'Cane Toads are toxic and Red-bellies are frog eaters, so they were eating the toads and being poisoned. Now over the years, they have started to diversify their diet, started to eat things like mice and lizards and, I think, they have learnt to leave toads alone.'

There must be something to this theory, because Tony now catches five or six Red-bellied Black Snakes every week, even in regions with high Cane Toad populations.

Despite being a venomous and potentially dangerous snake, there are benefits from having this species around your property. As well as eating frogs, lizards and sometimes rodents, Red-bellied Black Snakes are cannibalistic. They eat other snakes. And while not always the case, Tony tends to find areas with high concentrations of this species do not have too many really dangerous snakes, such as Eastern Browns, around.

Fact Sheet

Green (Common) Tree Snake

A very common Australian snake species, often mistaken for something more sinister than it is.

Identification: A thin-bodied snake, which can grow to almost 2 metres. The most common colours are olive green above and yellow below, but not always. With large eyes for their head size, these agile snakes are great climbers, but are also found on the ground and around water.

Diet: Primarily a frog-eater. This is a Colubrid (meaning rear-fanged) species that is non-venomous.

Where found: Common along the entire east coast. If you live in Sydney, Brisbane, even as far north as Darwin, you are likely to encounter this guy.

Tony says: A very common snake. Check out the range of colours in this bunch — from yellow/olive to green and even blue. They can also be orange, grey or even jet black. These cheeky fellows are not venomous, but they will bite if harassed. They are a very visual species and tend to rear up when someone approaches. This isn't a sign of aggression, they are just checking you out! The worst thing for me is the stink they give off when I handle one. Oh, by the way, some people call them 'Yellow-bellied Black Snakes', but they are not even closely related to the black snake family.

Green Tree Snakes

Green Tree Snakes

Fact Sheet

The Red-bellied Black Snake

This venomous snake is one of the most commonly encountered by humans across Australia.

Identification: Grow to approximately 2 metres in length, with a shiny black body, distinctive red side scales and a pale cream or pink belly. Some individuals also have cream or brown face markings.

Diet: Red-bellies primarily eat frogs, reptiles like lizards, and even other snakes. They are venomous and potentially dangerous, especially to the elderly, young children, or people with pre-existing medical conditions.

Where found: Common along the east coast, including Sydney, Brisbane, Melbourne, Canberra, Cairns, and as far west as Adelaide.

Tony says: I often find these guys in backyards, especially near water. They are often more active in cooler weather, compared to other snake species. Though they are venomous, they are not aggressive and would much rather flee than confront a human. They have small fangs, so one way to stay safe out in the garden is to wear thick trousers, boots and gardening gloves. If you see this guy while out in the bush, move slowly, stay well clear and you will find that in almost every instance, they will see you and move away. If you see one on your property and are worried, don't try and deal with it yourself, call an expert snake handler or your local wildlife authority.

Red-bellied Black Snake

Chapter 6

The Truth About Snakes

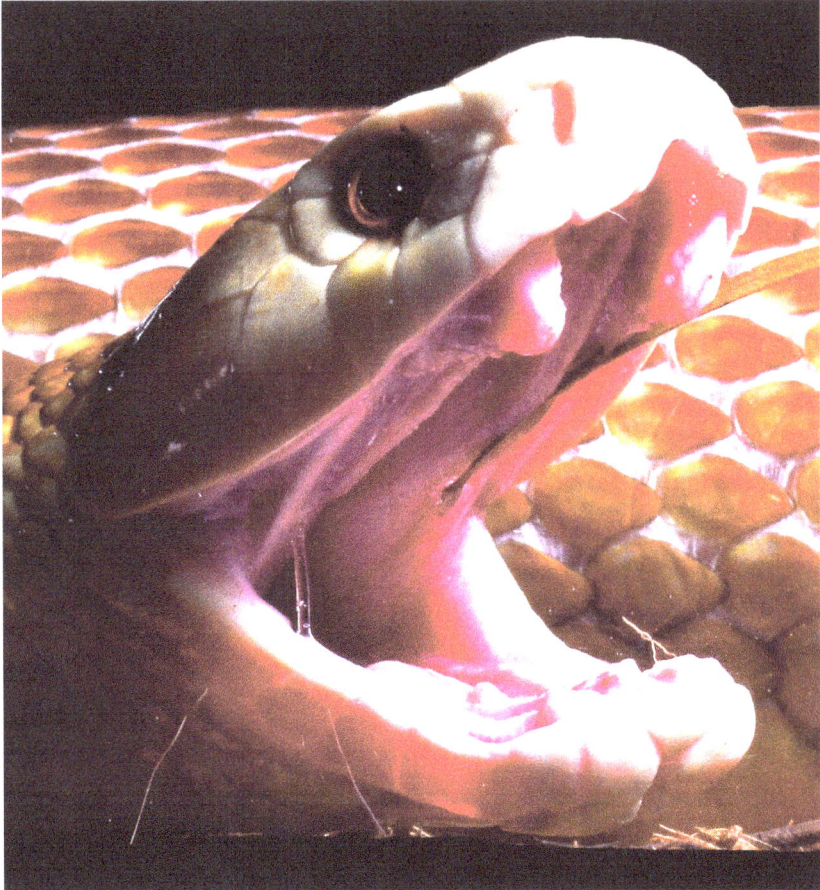

Since the beginnings of history, humans and snakes seem to have been in conflict. If you've ever read the Book of Genesis, you'll know the devil himself is represented by a serpent — a wily and evil creature — that God banishes to slither on the ground and strike at the heels of mankind for all time. Other cultures worship or demonise snakes as possessors of great power, magic, or evil. And still today, there are endless myths and stories about these misunderstood animals. So are any of these myths true? What are these ancient creatures really like?

The one that I find most confronting is that snakes are, by their nature, inherently evil beings. It's complete nonsense. Snakes are no more or less evil than any other living creature. They exist to eat, take shelter, sleep, and pass on their genes to the next generation. And, despite the Hollywood hype, snakes have no inclination to stalk and attack pretty girls, they are incapable of entering and possessing human bodies, nor are they inclined to wreak havoc on aeroplanes.

The other term that riles me is that snakes and other reptiles are 'cold-blooded', with the inference being they are callous — as we would say of a 'cold-blooded killer.' Now, if I remember my high school biology lessons correctly, reptiles are 'ectothermic', which means they need external sources of heat to warm their blood, to then become active. By contrast mammals, like we humans, are 'endothermic'. We generate our own heat through the processes of our bodies. Reptiles can't do this, so if the weather is cold, reptiles are cold and sluggish, but if the weather is warm, a reptile can be as hot-blooded, fast and active as any mammal.

OK, having got those off my chest, I check with Tony to see what myths bother him the most. He has quite a list.

~ ~ ~

Because humans and snakes have been at loggerheads for so long, perhaps it's no surprise that we've come up with so many snake myths over the years. Tony Harrison has heard plenty. Some are born of our fear, some are potentially very dangerous, and some ... well, they're just plain weird.

Many snake myths revolve around that most evocative of features: the flickering forked tongue. Snake tongues are not poisonous. A snake's tongue will not sting you, nor do snakes possess hypnotic powers through use of their tongues.

'The snake's tongue is its main sensory organ,' Tony explains. 'Just like we sense smell with our noses, the snake uses its tongue to collect particles from the air, then it runs its tongue across an organ on the roof of its mouth called the Jacobson's Organ. This organ is attached to the snake's brain, it analyses the particles and tells the snake whether it is approaching animal, vegetable or mineral.'

Sometimes you may notice a snake waving its tongue up and down. It isn't trying to hypnotise you, or lure you to your demise. As Tony says, it is collecting those particles from the air to sense its surroundings. Now a number of snake species, such as the Death Adder, do use a lure to attract prey, but this is located on the end of the tail and not the tongue.

A potentially deadly myth that Tony hears regularly is much more concerning.

'I hear people say all the time, you don't have to worry about baby snakes, because the venom isn't as strong. OK, here are the facts: there are some snake species which have a special protein in their saliva that enables them to paralyse and break down prey. We call this venom. Each species of venomous snake has its own venom characteristics. Some are more dangerous to humans than others. However, a drop of venom from a small or juvenile snake is just as toxic as that of a full-grown adult of the same species. The only difference is an adult has larger fangs and delivers more venom. So, if we consider something like an Eastern Brown Snake; a single drop of its venom can potentially kill many many humans, no matter how big or small the individual snake is. As a snake catcher, I often find the smaller the snake, the more dangerous it can be. Baby snakes are often more likely to strike and bite you, as they are little and feel threatened. Bigger animals may rely on their size to bluff and see off a predator.'

Let's be really clear then: in the snake world, size does not matter. It's the species that counts. Do not assume a small snake is less venomous than a larger one.

And it's important to know the species. This leads us to another dangerous series of myths surrounding snakes.

'Never judge a snake by its colour or its markings,' Tony says. 'People say all brown snakes are deadly, but that isn't true. As we've already seen, Green Tree Snakes can be brown, and they are harmless. Keelback or Freshwater Snakes (*Tropidonophis mairii)* are another species which are predominantly brown and are totally harmless. At the same time, Eastern Brown Snakes are often brown and are deadly, but they can also be orange or grey or black. If you see a snake, and don't know what it is, then leave it alone, or call an expert to deal with it.'

'Oh by the way,' Tony adds, 'the bloke up the road with a skin-full of courage, after downing fifteen schooners of beer, is not an expert … even if he says he is.'

Another common myth is that a snake with patterns on its skin is always harmless.

'Not true,' says Tony. 'Pythons are patterned and non-venomous, but a big specimen, like an adult Carpet or Amethystine Python can rip a decent chunk out of your arm with those needle-like teeth. In my book that's still dangerous. I've also seen snakes like Eastern Browns that are heavily patterned or striped, and they are the second most venomous land snake on earth. Stephen's Banded Snake *(Hoplocephalus stephensii)* is another highly venomous species with patterns on its skin. In Sydney, the Broad-headed Snake (*Hoplocephalus bungaroides*) is a venomous species that has a very similar skin pattern to the Diamond Python, which is a non-venomous relative of the Carpet Python.'

Once again, the message is clear — don't guess. If you don't know what you're doing, if you're not experienced, leave snake handling to the experts.

~ ~ ~

Many rumours, tall-tales or myths about snakes are born of our fear of them. And there are those that seek to profit from those fears.

'I'm often asked about keeping snakes out of people's property,' Tony tells me. 'The best method is to do the things I've already mentioned — keep your yard clear of rubbish and hiding places and don't leave food around to attract rodents. You can keep most terrestrial — or ground dwelling — species out by fencing your entire property with fine mesh, such as mouse wire.

But look, I've done tens of thousands of snake calls and there is no perfect method. I can honestly tell you, laying rope at the end of your driveway, or pouring diesel, Epsom salts, or chlorine around the perimeter of your land, will not stop snakes entering.'

Nor does putting out a saucer of milk attract a snake. 'Mind you,' Tony adds, patting his belly, 'if you do see a snake and you want to put out a saucer of milk, give me a call and then break out the Milo, 'cause I love the stuff.'

There are also a range of 'snake repeller' products available for sale in the market, and these are supposed to keep snakes away. Tony is certainly not convinced.

It's a warm spring day in Merrimac. A lovely day to be out and about, but Tony is not in the best of moods.

'This is one of those days when I need to duplicate myself,' he says. 'I have a line up of customers on the phone, all wanting me at their places immediately, plus I have a media film crew in tow, taking some footage.'

The man in the GPS starts giving Tony directions.

'The customer in this case speaks broken English, so I hope I have the address right, anyway, they are panicking because there are a couple of red bellies 'mating' in their yard. So this one could be interesting.'

Tony manages to locate the property and asks the customer to point him in the direction of the snakes. The first animal, a large male Red-belly Black Snake is curled up near a parked car and is an easy catch. But he's had a rough morning.

'Have a go at the bites on this guy.' Tony says. 'And you can even see venom on him. I don't think this was mating, I think this will be two males that have been in combat.'

He asks the customer; 'Was the other snake smaller than this?'

'Same size,' the customer replies, keeping his distance.

'Yeah. Two males fighting,' Tony confirms.

The media crew — using a small camera on the end of a very long pole — zoom in for some close-ups. The Red-belly isn't impressed. It starts biting at the camera — and then has a chew of Tony's boots. Like many Australian snakes, Red-belly Blacks have small fangs and Tony is in no danger of being bitten. He safely bags the first snake and then goes looking for the second.

The second Red-belly proves harder to find. He has taken refuge among piles of building materials and equipment. Tony begins to search and this is when he discovers several green mushroom-shaped devices stuck in the ground around the yard.

'Snake repellers,' he tells the camera crew. 'They vibrate and are supposed to keep snakes away, but as you can see, here we have two Red-belly males fighting over territory where these devices are being used. What might that tell you?'

Eventually Tony finds the second Red-belly Black. It's another huge male, hiding beneath a ride-on lawn mower, and it too has bite marks and venom on its head and body. The film crew are impressed, especially when this snake attacks their cameras with even more vigour than the first.

'Because we've interrupted their fighting, they're pretty grumpy,' Tony says to the crew, before continuing.

'I've been to many, many clients with these so-called snake repellers installed, only to catch and remove snakes from their homes — and that includes all different species. These units vibrate and that is supposed to scare snakes away. But in nature, many things vibrate — trees in the wind for instance. It worries me that people are lulled into a false sense of security, and they then start walking around their backyards in bare feet and shorts, thinking they're perfectly safe. I mean, I've found snakes lying next to repellers, or on top of repellers. I've even found snakes mating or fighting over territory right next to one of these units. I have dozens of videos on YouTube showing these things.'

Anyway, we aren't here to put people out of business, nor are we stating these devices don't work. However, they are quite expensive to buy, and may lull a home owner into a false sense of security. As for their effectiveness ... well ... go and watch Tony's YouTube videos, do your own research, and we'll leave you to decide. In the meantime, take precautions when you are in potential snake territory.

~ ~ ~

There are other reptile myths that are just plain bizarre. Thankfully, not too many people believe these things anymore. Stories of snakes biting themselves to commit suicide, or holding onto their tails to roll down hills like a cart wheel — are mostly dismissed as fallacy. Tony still hears some beauties though.

'I still hear stories about mutant snakes,' he chuckles. 'People tell me they've heard of Green Tree Snakes that have cross-bred with Taipans to form these deadly tree-climbing mutants. Or Brown Snakes cross-breeding with Carpet Pythons to form giant super snakes. Look, it can't happen. It's not biologically possible. It's like saying a human could mate with a monkey to produce a cross-breed.' Then he adds; 'mind you, I have some mates who might want to try that after a few schooners...'

That, I suspect, is a story for an entirely different book.

~ ~ ~

The important point to remember is this: these myths do little to properly educate the public on the truth of reptiles, especially snakes. By learning a few facts, we hope people begin to understand that snakes are not evil, mindless killers, bent on the extermination of the human race. In fact, snakes often have a lot more reason to fear us than the other way around. Still, playing with dangerous reptiles every day can come at a price.

In the next chapter we will begin to understand the dangers of dealing with potentially deadly snakes, and some of the other reptile species. This is a situation Tony faces whenever he goes to work, or when he opens the enclosure door to one of his pets.

If Bitten

If you do happen to be bitten by a snake, there are some other myths Tony would like to correct. Get some simple things right, and you stand every chance of making a full recovery, even from the bite of the most venomous species.

'Firstly,' he says, 'unless you are completely sure of the species that has bitten you, assume that every bite is a venomous one. Do not cut the wound. Don't try to suck out the venom. Don't apply a tourniquet or cut off the circulation to the bite area. What you do is leave the bite area unwashed, and then apply a compression bandage over the bite site. Then continue to wind out the bandage along the area of the body where the bite has taken place, such as the arm or leg. This bandage should be wound as tight as you would apply for a sprain. Don't try and cut off blood supply. If you have a pen or pencil or some other sort of marker available, put a cross on the bandage where the bite is. This will allow medical staff to examine the bite site without removing the entire bandage and freeing the venom. Very importantly, you should stay as calm as you can. I know you will be afraid — that's natural — but it is important that you don't go running around. Venom travels through the lymphatic system of our bodies. The more active you are, the faster the venom travels. Apply a compression bandage to slow the movement of the venom and call triple zero to get to hospital.'

We recommend you get the full information, including a fact sheet on snake bite first aid, from the St John's Ambulance website.[1]

---

1   www.stjohn.org.au

Fact Sheet

Brown Tree Snake

Common in the warmer areas of Australia, the Brown Tree Snake is sometimes called the Night Tiger. However, it is not closely related to the highly venomous Tiger Snake family.

Identification: Brown Tree Snakes can grow up to 2 metres long. They range in colour from apricot to very dark brown and may have flecks or stripes across their back. They have huge eyes, a large head and cream or salmon-coloured belly.

Diet: These snakes eat birds and bird eggs, as well as frogs and lizards and small mammals. They mostly hunt at night and rest during the day. Venomous, but not considered dangerous.

Where found: Right across Northern Australia and down the East Coast as far as Newcastle. Common in cities like Brisbane, Cairns and Darwin.

Tony says: These guys are quite defensive and tend to strike first and ask questions later. This can shock people, especially when they see a snake with stripes. In Queensland they have the nickname 'Night Tiger', which also leads people to think they are deadly. In fact, Brown Trees are colubrid, or rear-fanged snakes and while they do have venom, it only has a similar intensity to a wasp or bee sting. Also, they have to chew on you to inject their venom, so if you keep your distance, you have little to worry about. These guys love to climb and I often find them snoozing in people's eaves or garden gazebos. They hunt birds and I sometimes find them trapped in bird cages or aviaries with a belly full of budgie. As with any brown-coloured snake, if you're not sure of its identity, assume the snake is dangerous, leave it alone and if concerned, call an experienced snake catcher.

Brown Tree Snake

Brown Tree Snake

Fact Sheet

Keelback or Freshwater Snake

The Keelback is a common visitor to backyards in the warmer parts of Australia, especially where there is water nearby.

Identification: A fairly small species, the Keelback can grow up to 1 metre in length. They range in colour from grey or olive, to brown, and even almost black. Most have mixed flecks of dark and pale colour on their scales, sometimes in bands. The snake earns its common name from raised keels through each scale on the back and sides. These keels act like the keel of a boat, helping the snake to move through the water.

Diet: Primarily a frog eater, this snake is something of a conservation legend as they are one of the few animals that can eat the invasive Cane Toad without suffering the effects of the toad's poisonous skin glands.

Where found: Keelbacks live in tropical and sub-tropical Australia, from Northern NSW, to the Kimberley in WA. They are common in places like Brisbane, Cairns and Darwin, usually in areas with water.

Tony says: If you have fish ponds, or a pool or a watercourse near your place, you may well have these cheeky fellows around. I catch a lot of these guys in and around the Gold Coast — even in built up areas.

Though non-venomous, there are two major issues with this snake. First, it can be hard to tell him apart from another, similarly coloured — and highly venomous — species called the Rough Scaled Snake. Keelbacks are often found in muddy situations, so identification can be really tough if you don't know what you're doing. Second, even for experience snake handlers, this guy gives off the most disgusting odour when handled.

Keelback Snake

Chapter 7

Sometimes it gets Dangerous

Buccan is a semi-rural community at the northern end of the Gold Coast, south-west of Brisbane. There are small acreages and rolling paddocks. Signs out for horse manure and Bobcat hire. It's November, overcast, but warm. Tony Harrison has been called here by a lady with a snake problem. She heard her dog growling inside the house, and when she went to investigate, there was a snake tail vanishing into her bedroom. She couldn't tell what it was, so she shut the snake in. She put a towel under the door to stop it escaping. Then she called Tony.

It's a good day for just about any snake species; warm, but not too hot. And Buccan, according to Tony, is 'Snake City'. He turns off the narrow bitumen, onto a property with wide green paddocks, walls of eucalypt trees, animal feed and long corrugated iron sheds. It's a five star serpent resort. Tony has a bad feeling.

The lady owns a brick home, neatly kept, with a wraparound verandah. Tony is greeted at the back door by the lady and her little grey dog. She leads Tony down a long brick-walled hallway to a heavy red timber door. It's dark. Tony switches on a torch. The towel is still wedged under the door, to keep the snake in one place.

Tony swings open the door. It's a bedroom, airy and bright, chestnut timber furniture, pink soft furnishing, and grey carpet ... with a huge snake poo sitting in the middle of it.

'That's probably a good sign,' Tony tells the lady.

The lady wants to know how on earth the snake could have got into her house. Tony shows her the gaps around the windows and up into the ceiling. Snakes can fit through gaps one-third the size of their body width. There are plenty of places in this room where a snake could squeeze in, or escape. Tony wonders if it hasn't already left. Buccan is a decent drive from his place. A long way to come for nothing. But there is that huge poo...

Tony starts searching around the corners of the room, shining his torch down under the long drapes and behind the bed. Nothing. There is a pink lounge chair beside the bed, with a large floral cushion sitting on it. Tony shines his torch around the base of the chair and underneath. Still no sign. It's not looking good. But then he lifts up that cushion.

Kah-boom!

An Eastern Brown snake. Big. Close to two metres long.

It's curled on the cushion of the chair. Curled right where a person would have sat.

'Have a look at this,' Tony says, beckoning the lady a little closer. 'Imagine if you'd sat down on that lounge. Do you know what it is?'

'Is it a Brown?' the lady asks.

'Yeah, bloody oath it's a Brown. If you'd sat down on that chair that thing would have nailed you ten times before you'd be able to get out again.'

'Oh bloody hell...' the lady says after a deep breath; taking in the seriousness of the situation.

The snake begins to uncoil itself, tongue flickering at the torch beam, realising its cover has gone. It starts to jump and twitch and quiver — in that way Eastern Browns do.

'Every now and then I do a job which really could have been disastrous,' Tony says, 'and this is one of them.'

He uses a pillow to hide the Eastern Brown's face and then lifts it off the lounge by the tail. The snake isn't impressed. It starts to strike at Tony's shoe.

Strike and retreat. Strike and retreat. Strike and retreat.

This is an Eastern Brown tactic. Tony is expecting it. He knows these snakes well. His thick pants and shoes save him from being bitten by the world's second most venomous land animal.

'He's a biter,' Tony tells the lady, perhaps unnecessarily. 'That's the third time he's nailed me already. If that'd been you sitting on him on that chair, I reckon you'd have been on the news tonight.'

This is the perfect example of the dangers of dealing with venomous snakes. A close call, but one with a happy ending. It's the reason why Tony insists people should ring an expert if they see a snake inside their house. And why one lady in Buccan is alive and well, thanks to some common sense — and the keen eyes of her little dog.

'There was another job, a year or so ago,' Tony remembers. 'In Coomera. A lady called me about a snake in her bathroom. I walked into this dark room, didn't see a snake anywhere, but I sure felt one.'

Tony had a small, and very angry, Eastern Brown Snake hanging onto the leg of his pants. Once again, being appropriately dressed saved him from a hospital visit.

'I was OK, because of what I was wearing, but that lady was wearing shorts and thongs,' Tony tells me, 'if she'd gone into that bathroom instead of me, she'd have been bitten for sure.'

Venomous snakes — especially Eastern Browns — seem to share our passion for the beach. Tony often receives calls to come down to one of the many Gold Coast beaches to remove an unwanted sun-seeker.

'The danger in these situations is that you have a bad combination of factors,' Tony says. 'First you have nice warm weather, which means people head down to the beach, wearing bathers and flip-flops, even bare feet. At the same time, the warm weather means snakes are active too, and an Eastern Brown down at the beach is likely to be very warm and super-charged. I've had instances on the Coast where people have been lying on their towels, sun-baking, only to open their eyes and see a snake right beside them, with its head popping out of a crab hole. We've had people stepping on snakes down on the beach. I guess when you think of snakes — maybe aside from sea snakes — you think of the bush, rather than the beach, but this is a timely reminder that snakes can be anywhere and people should always keep their eyes open.'

~ ~ ~

The fact that Tony continues to head out each day to capture and relocate deadly snakes like Eastern Browns seems remarkable to me. His calm demeanour amazes me even more. Considering one came close to putting him in a pine box. I ask Tony about what happened.

'I can even remember the exact time and date,' he says. 'It was a regular customer of mine called Jim. He called me at 11:10am on 2nd September 2007, to tell me he was on a job on Sovereign Island and that he had a brown snake. He told me it was big bugger, and for Jim to say that, I knew it was going to be a huge meat-axe of a snake.'

'I don't live too far away, so it didn't take long to get over there. And when I arrived I found this bloody huge Eastern Brown — it was easily six foot long — which had travelled over to the island in a truck full of dirt from Reedy Creek. So after being picked up, driven around and dumped out of a truck, it was pretty pissed off.'

Tony explains to me that he caught the snake without too many problems. He bagged it and tied it up. Like most professional handlers, Tony uses calico catch bags to hold and transport captured snakes until they are released out in the bush. Except this particular bag was old, the fabric thin and worn, and it was a little too small to be holding a six-foot long Eastern Brown. Or maybe it was way too small.

'I got home and showed my daughter the size of the snake. It was pushing its head up to the top of the bag, into the knot I'd tied, close to where my hand was. Suddenly I felt it close its mouth over my finger. I realised what had happened and I'm sure I let out a few choice words. Then I asked my daughter to go and find her mum.'

I gather from Tony that there was a little panic in the household for a while there. Maybe there was a lot. Tony, however, seemed eerily calm — at least that's how the story is related to me. In any case, not every bite from an Eastern Brown involves venom injection. And the snake had been in a bag — albeit a very thin one. But this is a very dangerous species of snake. You don't take chances.

'I administered first aid on myself and then found the bloke next door and asked if he'd take me to hospital. As we were on the way, I called the hospital to tell them I was coming in and what had happened, so they were ready. When we arrived they took me in and whacked a cannula into my arm, starting the process.'

After about an hour and a half, a nurse came to check on Tony. She unwrapped the compression bandage to take a photograph of the bite site.

'My finger was really swollen,' Tony remembers. 'I knew then that I'd been invenomated.'

And then everything went horribly wrong.

'It only took a few minutes and I started to feel crook. Firstly it felt like I'd been busting to pee for hours. My breathing started to go; I was having trouble taking full breaths. Then my heart started pounding — each beat like a hammer blow to the head...'

Tony Harrison passed out. He had a seizure. He came close to death. Very close.

'About five hours or so later I woke up. I remember hearing the voices of Joe Sambono, Doctor Paul Masci and Doctor Darren Green — you know, I think these guys are the best in Australia — so that's when I knew it would be OK.'

They gave him ten vials of antivenin. He survived. And he went back to doing what he loves. He jumped right back on that horse.

'Twenty-six hours later,' he tells me, 'I was out in Beenleigh on another snake call. There I was, catching a Carpet Python in my PJs. I still even had my hospital arm band on.'

He's philosophical about the dangers.

'It happens. I have close calls pretty regularly — maybe a few times every year. They get the heart pumping I can tell you. But it's part of the job.'

Now I don't care what anyone says, in my book, that's one tough bloke.

~ ~ ~

There have been plenty of other potentially dangerous situations Tony has seen. He's found a Red-bellied Black Snake hiding in a toddler's cubby house and another in a wardrobe during a girl's slumber party. Then was the teeth-clenching case of a nocturnal and potentially deadly Eastern Small-eyed Snake (*Cryptophis nigrescens*) in a lady's toilet, hiding right beside the spare toilet rolls. Reaching down in the dark for another bog roll could have been a very unpleasant exercise. In each case, the home owners did the right thing and called an expert to deal with the problem.

~ ~ ~

Not every dangerous situation a snake catcher faces actually involves a snake. Tony's been bitten by plenty of other critters. He tells me a story about one of the worst.

'Yeah, I got fairly smashed by a big Lace Monitor *(Varanus varius)* a few years back. It was mating season and I'd caught a female Lacey at a customer's place and there was a big male there as well. I'd taped up the female — her jaws and legs — to make her safer to transport, but to start with, I didn't do this on the male. It was a mistake I guess, because — 'whack' — he got me big time. He was a big animal and he shook the hell out of me. And these guys have serious teeth. I was wearing thick jeans and a pair of long boots and he got me on the calf muscle. I felt the hit, obviously, but didn't realise how serious it was until I felt blood filling up my boot. I had a mate with me, so I rolled up my jeans and asked him how bad it looked. He kind of went pale...'

~ ~ ~

And the danger doesn't always end out on the job. When you own a menagerie of reptiles, including Fresh and Saltwater Crocodiles, your chances of being bitten every once and a while are quite high.

'Even the most placid animal, handled regularly, needs to be treated with respect,' Tony says. 'Especially around food time. I have some critters that I use in shows and handle regularly, and they are puppy dog tame, but when there is food around, their instincts kick in, and if you put yourself between them and the food, no matter how red-hot a keeper you think you are, chances are you'll be bitten.'

'Crocs are the worst,' Tony tells me. 'I was off my feet for nine days fighting off infections after my big Saltwater Croc, Kursid, bit me on the hand. I didn't think the bite was too bad, we had friends from interstate staying and I didn't want to pack myself off to hospital, but in a few hours I was starting to feel crook and my hand was a real mess. And the same thing has happened to me since with croc bites. It must be something to do with the bacteria in their mouths, on their teeth or in the water. Anyway, I when I got to hospital, the doctor was telling me the symptoms I would experience, almost exactly as they were happening. It was pretty bad. And it was really fast. These days, even with a small croc bite, I don't mess around. If I get a bite, I get it treated straight away.'

~ ~ ~

One final and potentially dangerous story sticks with me. It reinforces how a man's passion for his vocation can overcome almost anything. It's another snake call for Tony Harrison. It's late at night, in January 2013. There's a chook shed with an Eastern Brown Snake inside. It's dirty, dusty and an agitated Eastern Brown is hiding somewhere in the pitch black. Now remember, this is the same breed of snake that almost killed Tony a few years earlier.

He starts poking around in the dust and chook feathers, looking for this snake. It's oppressively dark. Tony has to work by torch light. Dust and chook feathers float luminous through the beam. There are sheets of tin and planks of wood everywhere. A million places for a snake to hide. Tony finds the snake, but can't tell the safe end from the dangerous one. And he has no idea how he's going to get the thing out. He starts lifting a large section of tin with the edge of a shovel. The chooks start clucking warily, but the snake has moved on. No doubt it's even more agitated by this point.

'Snake's not there anymore,' Tony snarls.

He starts to fiddle around and then...

'Oh yeah it is.'

There's a flash of dull brown scales in the torch light. The snake is wedged into a corner of the shed. There's room now for Tony to use the shovel to force the snake out of his hiding spot, but that could injure the snake. Instead, he finds a thin leafy branch from a bush and gently begins coaxing the snake out. He wiggles the branch. The snake starts becoming jumpy — twitchy and nervous, in that way Eastern Browns do — and the chooks cluck again.

Tony manages to find a coil in the snake's body, leverages the stick into it and slowly drags it towards him. A head becomes visible. Lots of agitated tongue action. Tony reaches into the darkness, beyond the light of the torch beam and pulls the Eastern Brown out. Chooks cackle as centimetre after centimetre of lethal reptile is revealed. Tony lifts the snake outside the shed and wanders over to where he has a catch bag waiting. I notice this bag is a newer one — the material is nice and thick.

'I see you've had a bad week buddy,' Tony says to the twitchy snake. He gently steers the Eastern Brown towards the catch bag. 'C'mon, a bit of refuge for you in there.'

After a few false starts, the snake slides compliantly into the bag and Tony ties it up.

'What a pain in the butt that was to catch,' he says.

'You made it look pretty easy,' the owner of the home chuckles, sounding a little like one of his chooks.

No doubt he's as impressed as I am at the gentle ease with which Tony can catch the snake he considers Australia's most dangerous — the species which almost killed him.

But it's not the potential danger that Tony's lamenting. Not the potential of another stint in hospital, absorbing anti-venom. He dusts off his jeans and shirt. He's clearly unhappy.

'I really really don't like getting chook poo on myself,' he says.

His attitude makes me laugh. Of all the things that his job presents, dirty jeans would be the least of my worries. Or maybe he's having a lend of us. And that's OK too. In a job like Tony's, it's sometimes good to have a laugh.

Protect Your Pets

Speaking of pets, the animals we keep — even those without scales — can become like members of the family. And these furred or feathered family members can face dangers from wild reptiles.

It's September 2013 and Tony Harrison has had the busiest winter he can remember. Warm dry days on the Gold Coast have seen snake activity continue, even during traditionally cold months. Tonight he's on the TV news again, reminding viewers that peak snake season is here, and it's here early. Featured in the news story are a Gold Coast family, who are counting their blessings after their pet Staffy confronted an Eastern Brown snake, was bitten, but managed to survive. The snake was in the family's vegetable garden — a popular place for their three young children to play — the dog saw the snake first, killed it, but was bitten himself.

'Dog fur offers reasonable protection from the short fangs of most Australian snakes,' Tony says. 'But they have such a strong sense of smell, a dog will typically investigate things face-first, and this means they can be bitten on the nose or tongue by a snake. Applying a compression bandage to a dog's face is virtually impossible, and even if you get it to a vet for anti-venom, with a snake like an Eastern Brown, one decent bite can potentially kill many humans, so a smaller animal like a dog is in big trouble. To survive a bite like that is very rare.'

Tony is often frustrated by people's attitudes to both their pets and wildlife. 'People set their dogs out to chase away or kill a snake. It's very dangerous for the dog. An Eastern Brown can do serious damage to a full-grown horse, so a dog is likely to die if it is bitten. Yet I regularly find dead or damaged snakes where people have set their dogs out to kill them. Often the snake is harmless and needlessly killed, but if your pet does happen to take on a dangerous snake, it can lead to a very unhappy ending.'

Cats too cause problems, and their owners sometimes put their feline friends in danger. Tony has seen dozens of cases of cats killing or being killed by snakes. 'Letting your cat out a night is inviting trouble,' he says. 'Not only does this place smaller nocturnal species in danger from cat predation, but big snakes like Carpet Pythons hunt at night. And to a big Carpet, a cat makes a very nice meal indeed. You wouldn't believe how many callouts I've gone to where distressed owners have just witnessed their cat being killed and eaten by a big Carpet Python.'

To prevent these types of tragedies, Tony recommends keeping pets indoors or in areas of the yard that are well-kept and where snakes are less likely to frequent. Cats should be kept inside, especially at night, to keep them safe from larger pythons and also to protect wildlife from being hunted.

To keep smaller animals, like birds, rabbits and guinea pigs safe, Tony recommends cages be solidly constructed, with lockable tops and doors — snakes like pythons can prize open unlocked doors and squeeze inside — and secured to the ground. They must be constructed using strong metal mouse wire or bird mesh — ideally with gaps smaller than 5mm, to prevent smaller snakes from entering. If possible, cages should be moved inside at night to keep smaller pets safe from nocturnal hunters like Carpet or Diamond Pythons.

Fact Sheet

Eastern Small-eyed Snake

A very little known, but relatively common snake. These guys bear a passing resemblance to the Red-belly Black snake and are potentially dangerous.

Identification: A relatively small species, these guys usually don't exceed 50cm. They are usually steel-grey to very dark brown above and they have a pink-cream coloured belly. They are a relatively placid and slow moving species.

Diet: A specialist lizard eater, these snakes hunt at night, foraging around rockeries and catching lizards as they sleep. They are venomous and potentially deadly to people.

Where found: Along the east coast from Cape York to Eastern Victoria. Common in higher rainfall areas, such as the Gold Coast Hinterland or mountainous areas around Sydney.

Tony says: These little guys are often mistaken for the Red-belly Black. However, there are differences. Red-bellies are usually jet black and have bright scarlet side and belly scales. Eastern Small-eyes are less dark and usually have dull pink or cream bellies. They are slow moving and fairly calm snakes. But don't be fooled. These guys pack a wallop. The medicos sometimes call them 'Meat Tenderisers', and for very good reason. They have venom similar to a spider — which causes muscle degeneration or necrosis. It's nasty stuff. I often find these guys in and around retaining walls or in cooler, moister places, such as pool-side rock gardens. They sometimes stray to the inside of garages, or cooler places in the house, like bathrooms or tiled areas. If you live along the east coast, it's wise to check your shoes before putting them on, and don't walk around barefoot in the dark, as these guys are nocturnal.

Eastern Small-eyed Snake

Eastern Small-eyed Snake

Fact Sheet

Lace Monitor

Monitors — or Goannas — are the largest lizards in the world. And one of the largest species, the Lace Monitor, is right at home on the fringes of our cities and even in our suburbs.

Identification: Large males can grow up to a maximum of 2 metres and weigh in excess of 10 kilos. They are mostly dark blue-grey to black with scattered yellowish spots and stripes. Some individuals have be more yellow than dark and in one form — known as Bells form — they have broad, black and yellow bands across the body and tail.

Diet: These lizards eat a variety of food, from insects to small mammals and birds. They are not adverse to scavenging from rubbish bins and picnic areas in parks and reserves.

Where found: Found from Cape York to South Australia. Common in National Parks and reserves on the margins of cities like Brisbane and Sydney. Occasionally found in suburban areas.

Tony says: These big fellows deserve the upmost respect. Although they are not venomous, they have serious teeth and claws and their bites can be especially nasty as they carry a lot of bacteria.

I sometimes find them raiding chicken pens for eggs, but really, anything edible and that will fit into that gaping mouth, is fair game. Generally, like most animals, they will run away from you if they can and these guys climb up trees like there's no tomorrow. However, as they become more accustomed to humans, they can become a nuisance. They will raid bins and try to steal your sausage sandwich at the local park. Give them space, because these lizards lose their fear and will readily defend themselves if confronted. And please, never feed them, as this can make the situation worse.

Lace Monitor

Chapter 8

You Just Have to Laugh

Case of mistaken identity? Is it a lizard, or something else?

I have a friend — let's call her Kate — who is terrified of snakes. Now, I don't just mean scared, I mean nuclear-strength terrified. She's terrified to the point where she won't visit our place anymore, because we own a pet python. She's terrified to the point where a rubber snake on the roof of her garage was enough to send her into hysterics. Even the 'Made in China' stamp on the red underbelly wasn't enough to convince her that the evil creature wasn't real and lying there waiting to sink its ridiculously oversized black rubber fangs into her yielding flesh.

Yeah, some people are really afraid of reptiles. And while we shouldn't mock the fears of others, some of the things Tony Harrison has experienced in 20 years of snake catching really are rather amusing.

~ ~ ~

Tony's out at midnight again. The roads are quiet. His driving lights turn grassy verges to the colour of beer — and I suspect a beer would go down quite well about now. It's going to be one of those nights. A customer has called him out to retrieve a very large Red-bellied Black Snake they've seen curled up on a rock in their garden. Tony smells a rat ... or maybe something else.

'Red-bellies are not normally nocturnal,' he says. 'I've seen it happen once, and that snake was forced out of somewhere. Anyway, I have the feeling this one is either dead, and someone's been playing a joke, or it's a toy.'

It won't be long until he finds out. The polite little man inside the GPS tells Tony he's reached his destination.

'I have a feeling it's going to be an expensive mix-up.'

Tony hops out of the car and strolls up to the house. He's greeted at the door by some fluffy dogs.

'Hey puppies,' he says.

'We're house-sitting for my mother,' a lady explains, as she unlocks the security door. 'I'm glad I saw this thing before the dogs went up to have a look.'

'It's very unusual for a Red-belly to be out at this time of night,' Tony warns, as they wander through the house. He's softening the lady up for possible disappointment.

'Oh, hopefully it's real and not a fake one,' the lady says, opening the back sliding door to let Tony outside again.

Perhaps she's prophetic.

Tony takes two steps out onto the patio and shines a torch light across to the distant rock garden. 'Uh-huh,' he grunts, good-naturedly, 'you want the good news or the bad news?'

'It's not a Red-belly?' the lady asks.

'Nope!' Tony replies. 'That's a toy.'

'What!' the lady squeaks, someone surprised.

Tony walks out to the garden, reaches into the rockery and picks up the offending critter.

'Oh, you're kidding me,' the lady says.

'Nup,' Tony replies. He walks back onto the patio and drops the toy onto a table. It makes a distinctly plastic sound when it lands. Though it's painted the colours of a Red-bellied Black Snake, it's not at all realistic up close.

'Who put that there?' the lady asks.

'Not me!' Tony assures her.

'I'm so sorry to drag you out all this way for nothing.'

'It's all good,' Tony says, 'I've seen it before.'

And he has...

It's summer in Tallebudgera Valley, a leafy area to the west of Palm Beach. It's typical of an area where man's activities continue to encroach into the natural world. That makes it a good place for snakes.

Tony Harrison is on his way to a family whose pet cat brought a snake in overnight. Based on the description given by the customer, Tony thinks the snake is a Stephen's Banded, a small and mostly nocturnal species, with dangerous venom that causes problems with blood clotting.

Tony takes up the story; 'Unfortunately the family cat was out at night, which it shouldn't have been, and it has brought the snake inside. Instead of calling someone for help, the customer took matters into his own hands, picked up the snake with a pair of kitchen tongs and tried to flush it down the toilet.'

However, this was one little snake that wasn't about to have its life flushed away.

'The chap came home from work next day, went to sit on the toilet, and got the fright of his life.'

Obviously the snake got a scare as well. It vanished into the workings of the toilet. The homeowner set to work on the plumbing. And he called Tony.

'So now the guy has taken his entire toilet apart — plumbing and everything,' Tony says. 'What should have been a relatively simple job just got a whole lot more complicated.'

When he arrives at the house, Tony is taken to the bathroom to find a toilet suite in several pieces, but the snake is nowhere to be seen. Assuming it is up in the rim of the toilet bowl, Tony asks for a hair dryer to heat up the area, which should gently encourage the snake out into the open. While the customer goes off to find a hairdryer and extension lead, his little boy wanders past the bathroom.

'The snake catcher is here,' the little fellow bellows in that much-too-loud way little kids sometimes have. 'So the snake go to hide in the toilet.'

That makes Tony laugh.

Meanwhile, the boy's dad returns with the hairdryer and a lead. 'I'm just really scared of snakes,' he says. 'That's why I flushed it. Y'know, I didn't want to kill it.'

'This is why you should call one of us,' Tony explains, starting up the hair dryer. 'See, this species of snake is a bit nasty. They have a venom which causes bad complications with your blood. Your limbs turn black, like you've been badly bruised. You can lose fingers and such. If you'd been bitten while you were sitting on the toilet, a certain part of your body would now look like a burnt sausage.'

'Oh, I'm gonna have nightmares now,' the customer says.

'The thing is, if you see a snake, just call an expert. It might cost you a little, but you'll have the peace of mind to know it has been safely removed and we can give you some tips on how to prevent it happening again.'

Tony eventually locates the Stephen's Banded Snake in the toilet cistern and makes a simple and safe capture. A little later, the snake is returned to the bush, hopefully to a future free from marauding moggies and toilet-related traumas.

~ ~ ~

In 20 years snake catching, Tony has seen some truly bizarre sights. Perhaps it's the unique Aussie sense of humour, or our paranoia about deadly snakes lurking under our very noses. It might be a combination of the two. Or maybe we've all watched too many of those B-grade snake movies.

'I've seen people put dead snakes in cars for a joke,' Tony laughs. 'Or rubber ones in beds. You name it. Everyone freaks out and then I get a call.'

There have also been some truly bizarre cases of mistaken identity.

'Mate, I've been called out to catch dog poo, radiator hoses, bits of rubber, insulation in cars ... I even remember a snake call when I found a steering wheel cover with two police officers standing nearby with hands on their guns.'

Tony's 'caught' snake skins, leaves and sticks which have been mistaken as snakes. He's found pieces of wire and even ... now how shall we put this delicately ... a lady's glow-in-the-dark, battery-operated 'self-help' device that someone thought was a deadly serpent.

There have been lizards too. 'Deadly' snake-mimicking lizards.

People are often embarrassed when they call a snake catcher, only to find that the 'Death Adder' out by the wheelie bins was actually a harmless Blue Tongue Skink.

Blue Tongued Skinks (Genus *Tiliqua)* are a common source of client calls. With their thick, snake-like bodies, camouflaged scales and relatively small legs, 'Blueys' are sometimes mistaken for snakes; especially Carpet Pythons, or the Common Death Adder (*Acanthophis antarcticus).* However, these lizards are totally harmless and will do your garden a favour by eating all those pesky snails.

Another lizard, the Eastern Water Dragons (*Physignathus lesueurii)* occasionally find their way into back yards and even swimming pools, and while not dangerous, they can pack a decent bite.

'Sometimes the males of this species get a little territorial and defensive,' Tony tells me. 'They may start trying to bite you, your kids or your pets.' If this happens, you may need to call a snake catcher or wildlife authority to help out.

~ ~ ~

Sex is a topic that generally gets people laughing. Sex in the animal kingdom is often a strange and, sometimes hilarious, world. But sexy reptiles? Really?

Far from being 'cold-blooded' when it comes to pleasures of the flesh, reptiles can be as determined, obsessive, and experimental as the hottest mammal. And just like we mammals, individual reptiles have individual personalities when it comes to love-making. There are the shy, the aggressive, the frigid, the compulsive, the downright peculiar.

One of Tony's pet Bearded Dragons is a fine example.

'He has a very over-charged sex drive' Tony says.

Right on cue the lizard starts scratching the substrate on the bottom of his enclosure, while the female sits nearby on a log, looking rather worn out. The little guy's hips start shuddering and wiggling as he rocks and rolls himself to paradise. The human males in the room nod sagely. Yep, it feels like we're sharing a moment ... secret men's business.

Homosexual behaviour is also fairly common in reptile life. Tony has his own gay couple of Gillen's — or Pygmy Mulga — Monitors (*Varanus gilleni)*. This small goanna species comes from the arid parts of central and north-west Australia. Originally, Tony had three of these beautiful little monitors, but unfortunately the female died. Tony thinks it was due to the constant sexual harassment she received at the hands of the males. Not to be deterred by the loss of their girlfriend, the two males went right on mating each other, with equal determination and vigour. So Tony re-named his happy little couple Miriam and Julian … you work it out.

'They're a happy gay couple,' Tony says. 'But this behaviour is not unusual, especially in captive animals. At the height of breeding time, males will, and this is a slightly delicate subject, rub up and down on other males, or on anything else they can find.'

'But it's not just males,' Tony continues. 'I have kept species such as Ridge-tailed Monitors *(Varanus acanthurus)* where the female has done all the leg work with mating. She will do all the wooing and the foreplay, and if she can't find the male willing to satisfy her needs, she would just as happily make out with another female. And it's not just lizards. I've kept Death Adders and Tiger Snakes which have shown similar sex drive during breeding season.'

Are you changing your mind about 'cold-blooded reptiles' yet?

Tony shows me into one of the larger cages. Two Taipans share the space. Or is it one enormous Taipan with two heads?

'Mating pair,' Tony tells me.

The male Taipan is much larger than the female. Tony has a love ballad playing on the radio — which is kind of appropriate. The two animals align their bodies, the male holding the female down. The male begins to twitch and flex his muscles, like the most amazing full bodied massage.

'That's how he woos her,' Tony says.

I believe it. It looks very enticing!

While we're on the subject of bodily functions, I can't believe how many people have asked me what snake poo looks like. It's a pretty funny question!

'If I'm out in the garden or bushwalking, how can I tell if what I see is a snake poo?' they will ask. 'I found this in the backyard, and I was worried it might be from a snake.'

OK, here goes: depending on the species, there are usually three components to snake faeces. First there will be the urine — or uric acid — which in snakes is secreted as white foamy substance that goes hard and chalky when dry. Then you have the brown faecal matter — the actual poo — and thirdly, you often have cast-outs, such as hair or feathers. Being a snake — as opposed to another shaped animal — snake poo is generally deposited in longer snake-like shapes. Makes sense?

By the way, sorry if you were eating while you read these pages!

~ ~ ~

OK, I'm convinced — even more than I was before — when it comes to our attitudes to reptiles, we've got it so wrong. Sexy snakes, desperate dragons and gay goannas. These animals experience some of the same feelings we humans do. The same urges. The same desires. We all eat and breathe. We make love and we go to the toilet. Maybe we humans are not as sophisticated as we like to make out!

~ ~ ~

As I've been working with Tony on this book, I've managed to hear more than a few funny quotes. This seemed like the right chapter to include them. No names, no pack drills...

Tony (*speaking to an audience during a Top Ten Venomous show*): 'If I had to say what species of snake I was most like, I reckon it'd be a Death Adder. I'm a short fatty and I prefer to sit around and have my food come to me.'

Tony (*explaining the captive husbandry for a monitor species*): 'I know people tend to keep these lizards at lower temperatures, but if you do, they end up as round as me ... and that's saying something.'

Customer (*speaking on the phone to her friend after Tony has caught a Green Tree Snake inside her house*): 'Sorry, I have to go. I want to take a photo of a snake and this nice man.'
Tony: 'Nice man ... I think maybe you need glasses.'

Tony (*speaking at a Top Ten Venomous show*): 'Now Australia has 23 of the 25 most venomous snakes on earth. Hah! I can see some of you tourists are ready to pack up and go home already.'

Tony (*speaking to family who have just had a Carpet Python removed from out the front of their restaurant*): 'This is more than likely a male Carpet Python, and he's out at the moment looking for females.'
Customer (*speaking to her brother*): 'Hey, just like you.'
Tony: 'Yeah, except the snake only gets it once a year.'
Customer (to her brother): 'Hey, just like you.'

Tony (*holding onto the tail of a particularly agitated Eastern Brown Snake he has just caught in a customer's kitchen*): 'This is not the sort of snake you want to have wandering around your house. This is the second most venomous land animal on earth.'

Customer (obviously upset and concerned): 'Oh gee!'

Customer's kid (obviously less concerned): 'Can I hold it?'

Fact Sheet

Common Blue Tongue Skink

These harmless lizards are sometimes mistaken for snakes, but if you take a little time to look closer, you might save yourself a scare.

Identification: Grow to about 60cm, with stout fleshy bodies and small legs. Variable in colour, from brown to grey or silver, yellow and cream. Can be blotched or striped. Bright blue fleshy tongue.

Diet: Invertebrates, including slugs, snails and other garden pests as well as some plants.

Where found: Over much of eastern Australia. Very common in backyards, even in major cities like Sydney and Brisbane. Other Blue Tongue species are found across the country.

Tony says: A great snail catcher, these guys are attracted to backyards to eat your garden pests. And while they can bite, Blueys have blunt teeth and rely largely on bluff to surprise a predator. They will hiss like a snake, throw open their mouth and stick out that bright blue tongue. People sometimes mistake them for snakes. However, if you take a little time, keep a safe distance and then observe, you can save yourself an unnecessary call to a snake catcher. When it comes to telling lizards from snakes, there are three things to look out for. First, lizards have legs or residual legs (in the case of legless lizards). Secondly, unlike snakes, lizards can hear and have visible ear holes on the sides of their head. Finally, and this is the clincher, aside from goannas, lizards have thick fleshy tongues, like a human or a dog or cat. Snakes have specialised, narrow tongues with a fork on the end. If you're still concerned, call your local wildlife authority or reptile catcher for help.

Blue Tongue Skink

Fact Sheet

Eastern Water Dragon

A common sight, this big dragon is often heard rather than seen. They have a habit of basking over a creek or river and 'plopping' themselves into the water when danger approaches.

Identification: Grows up to 80cm. They are grey or brown in colour and sometimes have bands or stripes on the body. A distinct black band stretching from the eye towards the rear of the head. Males develop intense red — orange colouration on their chests.

Diet: Water Dragons eat anything they can fit into their mouth, including insects, spiders, frogs, smaller lizards and even small rodents.

Where found: Along the east coast, from Sydney to North Queensland. Common in built up areas of major cities like Sydney and Brisbane.

Tony says: I often find these guys around pools or ponds in backyards. They are generally no problem to people, but occasionally I get calls about an aggressive one. Males are very territorial and in the breeding season will not tolerate other males. Sometimes this extends to dogs, cats, and even people. And while they are not venomous, they are powerful lizards and can inflict nasty wounds if mishandled. They have a good set of teeth and very sharp claws. The best advice is to just leave them alone and let them move off at their own speed. If you have a territorial male that's causing problems, call an expert to come and deal with it. And please, don't feed these, or any other reptile, as it can lead to dependence and aggressive behaviour.

Eastern Water Dragon

Chapter 9

Late Calls and Pitfalls

It's early morning, January 2013, an hour when most of us are lost to sleep, and a lonely 4WD is rolling along a Gold Coast Highway. Rows of street lights flash past. The centre line glows. No one else is around. We see the lights of the dashboard.

'Déjà vu,' the driver huffs.

Tony Harrison is in familiar territory.

'Welcome to the Gold Coast,' he says, quoting a passing road sign. 'Yeah ... that's it. My boat's still out and ready to go. This is my fourth attempt to go fishing,' he tells the camera. 'I usually wake at 3:30, leave at 4. But here I am, ten-past-friggen-one and what am I doing? I'm out catching snakes.'

~ ~ ~

During the busiest times of the year, snake catchers like Tony Harrison have very little time to themselves. And on the Gold Coast, the busy season starts while it's still winter. In fact, Tony's busiest ever day was in August 2012, when he completed fourteen snake callouts in a single afternoon. The winter of 2013 was equally busy, with warm weather and plenty of snake activity.

'Heading out of winter is breeding season,' Tony explains. 'The female Carpet Pythons are in ovulation and it's the male's one shot at getting a mate. So they go wandering and people see a lot more of them. People see more snakes, and bingo — I get more snake calls.'

Things then remain busy right through until Easter, or sometimes even later.

'There are days when I hardly have time to eat,' Tony explains. 'When it's really busy, I can receive calls at any time of the day or night.'

'There are times when I need to split myself in half,' Tony grumbles.

Customer calls can be fraught.

'You have to understand, people's emotions can be running high. They see a snake and panic can set in. They make a decision to contact me, and once that's done, they want me there immediately,' Tony says. 'Unfortunately, I have to cover a lot of territory. The Gold Coast is a big area — close to 1400 square kilometres. I can be travelling anywhere from the NSW border to the outer suburbs of Brisbane and then west out to the Hinterland and Beaudesert. I can't be everywhere at once. And I can't always drop everything to go and pick up another snake. I mean, I've had times where I've been standing in someone's backyard with an Eastern Brown wiggling on the end of my arm, talking on the phone to an irate customer who has a Carpet Python up a tree. They don't see what else is going on. All they know is: they have a snake in their backyard and they want it gone ... now.'

This raises an interesting issue.

~ ~ ~

Someone wise once said to me: 'Customers ... you can't live with them and can't live without them ... but one day I'd sure like to try.'

With tens of thousands of customer calls in the last two decades, I wonder how Tony feels about the issue.

'Sometimes a deadly snake is the least of my challenges,' he quips. 'One of the reasons I started *Reptile Relocation and Awareness* was just that — raising awareness. And it's a challenge I face every day. Customers can be a real problem sometimes.'

It's not only the aggravation Tony faces — he can handle that — it's the continuing problems of people taking matters into their own hands. Too often, someone, or something gets hurt.

'The majority of people are bitten by a snake when they try to harass or kill it,' Tony says. 'And an awful lot of harmless snakes are killed through ignorance.'

I ask Tony for an example. It doesn't take him long.

'I remember one job, another midnight one,' he tells me. 'I got a call from a very scared lady to tell me there was a brown snake on a table in her house and it was threatening her. I tried to reassure her it was almost certainly harmless — probably a tree snake or a Carpet Python — because Eastern Brown Snakes don't climb. I told her I'd be there in a few minutes.'

'So I drove like a lunatic to get down there, only to have her ring me when I was a few streets away to say not to worry, because her neighbour had come down and killed the thing with a baseball bat. I told her I would come and identify the snake for her, since I was close. And I decided to video the call, to highlight the sorts of issues I'm sometimes faced with. You know, to raise awareness.'

Tony arrived at the property. There were two ladies, who introduced Tony to their neighbour. He was naked except for a pair of board shorts, no shoes, and he was holding an extremely dead and well-beaten snake. A tree snake. It wasn't a pretty sight.

'The guy had killed a harmless snake,' Tony tells me. 'I tried to explain the morality and legality of what he had done. And look, I understand the ladies were scared, but tree snakes are very visual. What the people perceived as a threat was most likely just the snake rising up to survey its predicament. It's what they do. Anyway, that wasn't the worst of it. The bloke had a skin-full of alcohol, was wearing nothing but shorts, and he really put himself at risk trying to kill the thing. Grog slows your reflexes down, and it also artificially raises your levels of bravado. It's a killer combo. If that snake had been an Eastern Brown, I'd bet quids that guy would have been off to hospital — or worse. He could have taken a bite on the arms, legs, even his body or face. It could have been catastrophic.'

There were stern words. The bloke followed Tony out to the car once the job was finished. I ask Tony what happened after the camera was switched off.

'Things kind of escalated,' is all he will divulge.

Yep, customers ... can't live without them...

~ ~ ~

Sometimes a snake or other reptile just makes itself too difficult to catch. If you can climb a tree or slide into a tiny space, a big predator will find it hard to get you. So that's what many snakes do when a human tries to catch them. And when this happens, Tony really has to earn his money. He's been forced to empty garages, clear gardens, move furniture, pull apart decking, disassemble retaining walls, unscrew fittings ... the list goes on. In a single day of callouts he may need to take on a role as a removalist, gardener, carpenter, plumber, landscaper, demolition expert, mechanic, or almost any other trade you can name.

'A customer will see a snake, give me a call and in the meantime the snake disappears. And if I can't find it, or remove it, then the customer has no peace of mind. That's bad for the business and really bad for the customer. So you try to do whatever it takes to find the animal.'

Some jobs are really impossible — too difficult for even someone as experienced as Tony to make a successful capture. 'Roof spaces can be a nightmare. Carpet Pythons and Tree Snakes just love hanging out in people's roof space. The customer will see a snake go into their roof and they give me a call. Yet in the hot weather, a snake can dangerously overheat up in a roof, so they often retreat down into a wall cavity or into the eaves. The customer gets upset when you tell them 'yes, you have snakes in your roof', but 'no, I can't get them.' I try to explain basic physics — a snake can fit into places where a bloke with a big gut like me just can't go.'

Cars also present a major challenge. 'Cars are a real pain,' Tony says. 'Snakes like Green Trees and Carpet Pythons get up into body panels, engine bays or suspension components and they are almost impossible to catch. I remember a Green Tree Snake in an old Toyota a few years back. It was up in the front guard of this car and nothing I did would encourage it to leave. We put the car in the sun and started the engine in an effort to drive it out by heat. Every time the snake put its head out to look for an escape, someone would wander past or carry on, and the snake would disappear again. I parked the car next to some bush, hoping that might lure him out, but still no luck. Eventually I was able to go in after him, when he moved into a spot I could access from under the bonnet, but that was a real pain in the backside. That job took hours.'

~ ~ ~

Being bitten by a potentially deadly snake is a fairly obvious pitfall of a job like Tony's. As we've already seen, one came close to taking his life. But the threat of venom is not the only chemical hazard a snake catcher has to deal with. There are a number of species of snake who use both ends of the body to deter a predator. Biting is an obvious deterrent, but it's not the only way.

'Some of the snakes I regularly see have a habit of throwing out some hideously smelling chemicals to try and make you let them go,' Tony says.

I ask him for some examples.

'Green Tree Snakes are pretty bad. Carpet Pythons tend to pee or poo on you when you pick them up, which is never nice. I reckon Keelbacks are the ones though. I can scrub my hands for hours after I've handled a Keelback and I still can't get that stink out of my skin.'

We don't see Keelbacks down in Sydney. So, against my better judgement, I wondered what this chemical defence smells like. Tony has an answer for me. It's both articulate and awful at once.

'Imagine going to a childcare centre and collecting a whole day's worth of dirty baby nappies. Then put all those nappies in a sealed plastic bucket and leave them in the sun for a week. And then, open the lid and put your head into the bucket. That's kind of what it's like.'

But, believe it or not, there is something even worse than Keelback stench. And a warning here, gentle reader: if you're the squeamish type, it might be wise to skip this part and head to the next section.

A number of species of snake have another defence strategy when they are captured. Pythons in particular employ this tactic. Larger pythons often live a feast or famine existence. They may only eat a few really big meals per year. And a big meal, like a possum, swallowed whole, takes a python a lot of effort and energy to digest. Plus they have a huge lump swelling their belly, which slows them down. If they are feeling in danger they may regurgitate the meal to make good an escape. Tony often catches pythons in this situation.

'People see them after they've had a big feed and are out soaking up some heat to fuel the digestion process.' Tony says. 'Or they've just eaten the family's pet bunny or duck or something. They can be really stuffed, skin stretched like an overfull bag. Anyway, I come along, pick them up and put them in a catch bag and, in their distress, they throw up dinner.'

Snakes have incredible digestive ability. Because they don't chew their food, it is completely broken down by chemicals and bacteria in the animal's system. A large prey item, like a possum, that has been brewing away in that toxic soup isn't a very pleasant thing when it's vomited back up.

'Oh, I've had some horror stories,' Tony tells me. 'The catch bags are ruined and the whole inside of my car just reeks. One time it was so bad, I had to have my car professionally cleaned three times before I could drive it again, and the stink was still there. It's bloody awful.'

~ ~ ~

It's not just snakes that can create challenges. Lizards too, can create all sorts of pitfalls for people in Tony's line of work.

'Yeah, I've had my butt kicked by some lizards over the years,' he laughs. 'Skinks like Blue Tongues are OK, they're nice and slow, but the dragon and monitor species are lightning fast. You end up looking like a bit of a goose, hair-arsing along after this lizard, only to miss it by a mile. And even if you do get them, you often get a poor grip on them and they have a habit of biting. And some of the bites of these big lizards are really unpleasant, as you've already seen; one knocked my leg around pretty badly a few years back. A lot of them can climb too, and there's no way I can get my body up a tree to bring down a big lizard ... or a small one.'

~ ~ ~

Tony sometimes gets grief from outside his circle of customers. As is the case with other high-profile wildlife people, not everyone agrees with Tony's stance on protecting snakes. He receives plenty of dissent, and not always face-to-face. Unlike some other YouTubers, Tony does not disable comments on his videos. So he gets negative comments as well as positive.

One source of debate is the practice of releasing reptiles back into the bush. There are those who believe the practice puts the animals at risk, because it artificially inflates the numbers of species in the release site and introduces competition with local populations. Tony's reaction is simple:

'I comply with all the requirements of the authorities. I do the paperwork and detail everything about every capture and release. I always say to people; 'if you have a problem with the practice, please feel free to ring the authorities and register your complaint.' I even give them the names and numbers of people to call. I know it's not a perfect scenario. Most people acknowledge that. But you know, what's the better outcome? To give the animal a second chance in the bush? Or to have it killed by a human or a dog, or run over by a car. It's pretty obvious to me.'

~ ~ ~

There are other challenges to working in a job like Tony's. Things I'd never considered.

'I couldn't tell you the last time I went on a holiday — I mean a real holiday. Between my callouts and caring for my own animals, there just isn't time. I like riding my motorbikes and going fishing, but a planned trip can be cancelled with a few minutes' notice, because I get a snake call. I'm not complaining ... I wouldn't swap the life for quids ... but it's just a fact of life.'

'There's also the wear and tear on my gear.' Tony adds. 'I've broken more cars than a demo derby. Hundreds and thousands of 'klicks' every year. There are the speeding fines and the challenge of navigating around places. I reckon I know almost every street on the Coast by heart now.'

He does. Not only that, but he can often tell you what type of animal he's likely to find at a particular address, even before he gets there. That's what you get when you've spent the best part of two decades catching reptiles — and sharing your home with them.

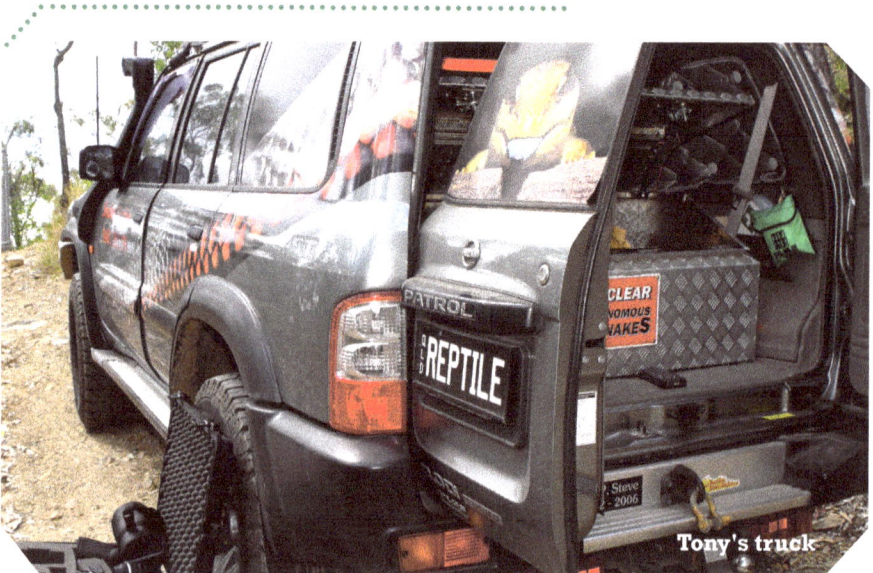

Tony's truck

Fact Sheet

Eastern (Mainland) Tiger Snake

An iconic Australian species, this potentially dangerous snake is becoming rarer in the north of its range. And there's a toad to blame.

Identification: Grow to around 1.5 metres in length. Extremely variable in colour, colour combination and patterns (see images). The most commonly seen form is dark olive to almost black, with cream or yellow banding. However, some may have no colour banding at all.

Diet: Frogs and lizards, but also mammals and even birds, depending on the locality and available prey.

Where found: South-eastern Australia from Brisbane and down into South Australia. There are also sub-species in Western Australia and Tasmania. Prefers cooler and wetter environments, such as the Great Dividing Range. Quite common around Melbourne.

Tony says: I very very rarely see these guys on the Gold Coast now. I believe there are some in the Hinterland area, but basically they have been devastated by the Cane Toad. While they are not often seen, Tigers have a very daunting defence posture where they flatten out their neck and head, a little like a cobra; they show their teeth and hiss away. It's quite a show. And it's worth listening too, cause these guys are dangerously venomous. Tigers prefer cooler areas, so if you live on the Great Divide, or are bush walking — especially in the cooler forests — you might see one of these guys. People in Victoria and Tassie certainly see them a lot more frequently than we do here in South East Queensland. Again, if you are concerned about one on your property, call a reputable snake handler or your local wildlife authority.

Eastern Tiger Snake

Eastern Tiger Snake

Fact Sheet

Common Death Adder

This snake is like no other in Australia. While it looks like an Adder or Viper, it is not related to these snakes and is an Elapid, like an Eastern Brown Snake or a Taipan.

Identification: Unlike any other Australian snake, Death Adders are short and thick and come in shades of grey or brown. They often have lighter coloured stripes but not always. The head is triangular shaped and the tail very thin and often a different colour to the body.

Diet: Ambush specialists, Death Adders lie under leaves and soil and use their coloured tails as a wiggling lure. They will eat anything attracted to the lure; birds, rodents, lizards or frogs.

Where found: Along the East Coast from the NSW/Victorian border to Cape York. Still common in areas around Sydney, but becoming rarer in Queensland. Other Death Adder sub-species occur across Australia.

Tony says: I rarely see these guys, mainly due to the impact of Cane Toads. But even where they are still common, people seldom Death Adders. They are not active hunters, but bury down into the leaf litter to wait for their prey to come to them. They can be very hard to see, which makes them potentially dangerous, as bushwalkers or people in their gardens can easily step on them. They are the fastest striking snake in Australia, with long fangs and very potent venom. If you are out in the garden, wear stout shoes and don't go burying your hands into piles of leaf litter or mulch — always use a spade or fork. If bushwalking, wear thick shoes, long pants and stick to marked tracks and avoid areas of thick ground cover.

Death Adder

Chapter 10

Tony's Home Zoo

I've always liked zoos. Over the years I've been fortunate enough to visit a few of the best. And while my 'Harry Butler dream' of being a zoo keeper never happened, I do work with a lot of zoo people here in Sydney, at the world famous Taronga Zoo. It's been a privilege to learn about the skill and dedication of these committed people. Keeping a large collection of animals in a healthy and happy condition is no small feat. They work long hours. They jobs are seldom glamorous. Yet their efforts are making a tangible difference to the plight of many endangered species around the globe.

Tony Harrison knows a thing or two about running a zoo. He has one in his house, under his house and in his backyard. At various times, Tony has kept close to 200 reptiles in his collection. And while he has cut back on his menagerie these days, watching him run through all the species he keeps is still like a reptilian roll-call.

'In there is a Striped Coastal Carpet Python,' he says, pointing at a glass-fronted, enclosure. He keeps moving and he keeps pointing to enclosures; 'another Striped Coastal; Striped Coastal; Striped Coastal; Collett's Black; Darwin Carpet; Darwin; Darwin; Diamond Python; Tiger Snake; Tiger; Tiger; Stimson's Python; Stimson's; Stimmy; Stimmy; Red-bellied Black; Death Adder; Western Taipan; Olive Python; Woma; Woma; King Brown; King Brown...'

On he goes. It's dazzling after a while. And it isn't just snakes.

Tony has kept a range of lizards, from large monitors to smaller geckoes. He has Blue Tongues and Shinglebacks. Outside he has a turtle pond and a larger meshed enclosure for his crocodiles. It's quite the menagerie. And everything is clean. All his cages are immaculate. His animals look great. If you ask him a question about a specific animal, he knows exactly what is happening with that animal. It's an impressive effort. And it helps you realise why, during those months when he's also catching snakes, Tony still has very little free time.

~ ~ ~

Subscribers to Tony's YouTube channel and social media sites are often asking for a tour of his facilities — to meet his animals. So I thought we should do that here as well. Here are some of Tony's favourites.

It's only right that we start with two of Tony's greatest loves — his two male Lace Monitors. Tiger was born in 2008 and came to Tony when he was about one year old. The guy who bred Tiger had already conditioned him to people and Tony has been able to use the big fellow in reptile shows, on TV, movie and photo shoots. He's co-starred with some of the greats. I mean, how many lizards can say they've worked with Gold Logie winner Lisa McCune?

Cyclops is a couple of years younger than Tiger. He is a 'Bell's Phase' Lace Monitor. Where Tiger has the traditional narrow, lacy bands of yellow and blue-grey, Cyclops has wide, heavy bands of colour, and is a very different looking animal.

Tiger and Cyclops both live upstairs at Tony's place and enjoy frequent romps around the house. Tony has to make sure he keeps his dogs out of the way when the big lacies are out. Dogs and goannas don't mix. They do however, share a taste in food. Cyclops in particular has a taste for dog kibble.

While both Tiger and Cyclops are extremely tame, they are still big powerful lizards, with sharp teeth and claws, and a heavy whipping tail. They are capable of inflicting horrific wounds. Tony needs to be on his guard when they are out of their enclosures.

'I remember a female friend coming over to visit once,' Tony tells me, 'and Tiger tried to climb up her and tore her top off.'

'The other thing you have to remember with monitors is that they are very food motivated,' Tony says. 'I have kept several different species, and they are all pigs when it comes to a feed. Even the little guys I use in demonstrations and kids shows are very different beasties when there is food around. If you get between a monitor and its dinner ... you can expect to be bitten.'

~ ~ ~

Another one of Tony's favourite pets was a big old Diamond Python called Brutus.

'Brutus had been around since dirt was invented,' Tony laughs. 'He lived for a long time in a cage I had in the backyard, with his multiple wives. Yeah, Brutus was a good old polygamous boy! Over the years I used him in shows, kids' parties and he was featured in a lot of photo work. He was in a music video with Peta-Evans Taylor — a song called *Inconvenience* — and he looked pretty good draped over her as she danced on the beach. I miss him. He was a beautiful old boy.'

Ironically, Brutus died back in March 2013, which was the very month he was featured in an '*Australian Girl's of Herpetology*' calendar, put together by the amazing photographer Shannon Plummer. Thankfully, through these videos and photographs, and through the animals he sired, memories of Tony's beautiful big old Diamond Python will live on.

~ ~ ~

A spectacular resident of the Harrison 'zoo' is Rocky the Red-bellied Black Snake. Rocky often features in Tony's snake shows. But even big stars sometimes have to face the realities of daily suburban life. One incident comes to mind. It's an example of how caring for reptiles is often a less-than-glamorous pastime.

It's a warm Gold Coast day and Tony is busy cleaning out his cages. Now snakes are cleaner and easier to look after than your average dog or cat. They don't make much mess and they usually don't smell. But every once and awhile they will do something like sliding through their own poo. And when that happens you may need to give your pet snake a bath. Today it's Rocky the Red Belly's turn.

Tony lifts Rocky out onto a concrete driveway, where it is sunny and warm and there's no dirt, which is important when a man wants to do a good job of washing his snake! Rocky lays out in that warm sun and you can almost see the contentment on his face. I swear he smiles! But then Tony comes back with a soaking wet washing brush. Gently, Tony runs the brush along Rocky's body, loosening off the crud and grime. Now Rocky is as tame as snakes ever get, but even the most placid animal can be upset at bath time. He rears up and puffs out his neck, not unlike a Cobra. It's classic Red-belly defence posture. His neck retreats into an s-shape and he even looks to be sizing Tony up for a bite. It's all bluff.

'Hey hey hey,' Tony chides. 'Piss off Rocky. Just calm down.'

Rocky retreats. He starts to look for somewhere to escape. It's what Red-bellies typically do when they are under pressure. But Tony hasn't quite finished the washing job. He gently takes Rocky by the tail with one hand and picks up the hose with another. A quick rinse off and the job is done. Rocky can now lie in the warm sun to dry. He looks shiny and brand new, and much happier now it's over.

~ ~ ~

Incredibly — considering he was bitten and almost had an appointment with the big snake house in the sky — Tony's pet collection also includes Eastern Brown snakes. One is a special, if occasionally ill-tempered lady called Jan.

'Jan was hatched out by a friend of mine,' Tony tells me. 'Fred was a great herp guy who passed away a little while ago. Out of 52 hatchlings that Fred produced, only two survived to adulthood. Baby Eastern Browns are notoriously difficult to get to feed, but Fred was able to raise two of them, and one of those animals was Jan. There are very very few genuinely captive-bred Eastern Browns in private collections, so Jan is a special animal to me. Anyway, I named her Jan, which is short for 'Not Happy Jan', cause she can be a bit cranky at times. Thankfully I have another Eastern Brown girl, called Isabelle. She's dog tame and I use her in my top ten venomous shows.'

As well as the bridesmaid, when it comes to the world's most venomous snakes, Tony also keeps the king. Number one on the toxic hit-parade. The Western Taipan or Fierce Snake is a seldom-seen resident of inland Australia. Drop-for-drop they are the most venomous land animal on planet earth.

'One drop of venom from these guys can take out 100 healthy humans,' Tony says.

Which I find sort of amazing, considering Tony has them living with him at his house. But Tony knows what he's doing. He understands how these snakes behave. He respects them.

He follows the rules. He takes precautions when working with these animals.

~ ~ ~

However, it's not just dangerous animals in this collection. Tony has kept harmless frogs, turtles and lizards as well. Two of his favourites are Mrs Fatbottom, a Shingleback Skink he uses for reptile shows and kids' parties, and a newer resident called Mr (Albi) Mangles, an albino Blue Tongue Skink. I notice the enclosures of both these lizards have unique husbandry features. Along with the usual logs and rocks and substrate and water bowls, there are squares of soft fabric.

'Those are their blankies,' Tony explains, which sounds kind of cute. 'Another keeper put me onto this tip and it seems to work. Blue Tongues and Shinglebacks — the bigger skinks — seem to feel more comfortable if they have a blankie in their cages. I'm not sure if it makes them feel more secure or what, and it kind of feels a bit silly for a reptile keeper, but it does seem to work.'

Tony also keeps a number of animals that his family have rescued from pet shops, because they were about to be euthanized. He has three-legged Bearded Dragons and other 'deformed' animals that the shops can't sell.

'We have a number of animals that were going to be put down,' Tony tells me. But my family, who have worked in pet shops over the years, always seize the opportunity to save the 'un-savable'. I've kept lots of snakes and lizards this way and I can't tell you how many times these animals — ones that were going to be killed — have lived healthy, normal lives, and some have even successfully bred!'

Fact Sheet

Yellow-faced Whip Snake

These guys are the Formula One cars of the snake world. A common, but rarely seen species, this little lizard hunter can move like there's no tomorrow.

Identification: A small thin snake, with individuals usually around the 60-70cm mark. Variable in colour, from blue-grey to shades of yellowish brown. Some individuals have copper-red streaks down their back. The belly is generally greenish-yellow. The most identifiable feature is the large comma-shaped mark which starts at the eye and goes down towards the mouth.

Diet: Primarily eats lizards, which it catches using its amazing speed. The bite from this snake is mildly venomous, but seldom dangerous.

Where found: Across Southern, Eastern and Western Australia. Found in cities including Brisbane, Sydney and Perth. Common, but not often seen.

Tony says: These guys are a bit of a nightmare to catch. They are so fast, they can make a snake catcher look a bit silly. I commonly find them in and around rockeries and retaining walls, where they hunt for lizards. And usually where I find one, there are more. They tend to be communal. As with most brownish-coloured snakes, these guys can be mistaken for juvenile Eastern Browns. The main difference is the big comma mark around the eye of the yellow-face Whip. Eastern Browns don't have this. These guys are venomous and have the potential to be dangerous. And while they prefer to run rather than bite, they will strike out in defence if they feel threatened. I can tell you, from personal experience, the bite of one of these guys hurts like hell. They may not kill you, but trust me, you'll wish you were dead. So if you see one in the bush or around your home, leave it alone and let it go on its merry way. And call your local snake catcher or wildlife authority if you are concerned.

Yellow-faced Whip Snakes

Fact Sheet

Marsh Snake or Swamp Snake

This frog-eater loves to live around water. Sometimes called the Black-bellied Swamp, or just Swamp Snake, these guys are mildly venomous and often mistaken for other species.

Identification: Grows to about 45cm, this small snake is variable in colour, from greenish brown to gun-metal grey, with dark scales on the belly. The most distinctive features of this snake are the two light-coloured stripes, one running towards the eye and another along the top of the jaw.

Diet: A frog and lizard eater. Marsh snakes are venomous, but not considered dangerous.

Where found: The east coast of Australia, from Sydney to around Cairns. Prefers moist areas such as around water courses and swamps.

Tony says: Another frog and lizard eater, these guys are fairly common and I find them quite a lot. They are mainly nocturnal, which means they sometimes fall foul of people's pet cats. The cat will often bring the snake inside, which isn't very good for the snake and not much fun for the owner either. Occasionally they will chase a lizard into a garage or house, which is where I catch them as well. While they are venomous, they are not dangerous and are very hesitant to bite. However, if provoke or if they feel trapped, they will bite and can cause some discomfort. To avoid confrontations with this little guy, be careful around ponds or water gardens and keep your pussy cat inside at night.

Marsh Snake

Chapter 11

Keeping Your Own Reptiles

Tiger the Lace Monitor

I'm sitting out in the back room of our house, watching an amazing natural sight. Our pet python is going through a shed. This is something all reptiles do. The process is quite astonishing. For several weeks now, the python has been off his food. Most of his time has been spent curled away in a hide, while his body pumps chemicals between the old skin and the new. At one point, he was temporarily blinded as these chemicals formed a milky bluish tinge across the scales covering his eyes. Now, on a warm November afternoon, he is shedding that old skin for good.

Unlike humans, who shed skin cells constantly, reptiles shed their skins in several large sections. Snakes generally will generally shed in one huge piece. The skin splits at the mouth and then the snake rubs itself against rough objects in its environment to begin breaking the skin free. Now, as I watch, our little pet python crawls out of the old skin like he's shedding an old translucent sock. It takes about 30 minutes. I spend that half-hour, sitting beside his enclosure, mesmerised at the sight.

Reptiles certainly can make fascinating pets. The number of licensed reptile keepers across Australia, and indeed the world, grows every year. Perhaps — in the same way Tony and I were inspired by Harry Butler — you're a young person who has been inspired by Tony Harrison to keep your own reptiles as pets. However, there are some things to seriously consider before racing out and setting up your own private snake house. You must do your homework. You need to get it right. It's important.

Remember, Tony is a guy who has kept reptiles all his life; 'And I'm still learning.'

First and foremost, the well-being of your intended pets must be considered. Different species of reptile have different care needs. Factors such as temperature, humidity, feeding and housing requirements must all be carefully considered. There are few vets who specialise in reptile medicine and those who do can be quite expensive to visit. However, many potential health problems can be alleviated by proper husbandry. If you plan to keep reptiles as pets, do your research. There are plenty of reputable websites and experienced keepers out there who are willing to help newcomers to the hobby. Tony Harrison is one of them.

Second, most reptiles are a long-term proposition. That cute little python you see in the plastic tub at the reptile expo or pet store — and just have to buy — will most likely live for 20 years or longer and may grow to two metres or more in length. Are you prepared for the investment, and the future needs of that animal? This is a good question to ask yourself *before* you hand over the cash.

Also, reptiles are not like dogs or bunny rabbits. They are not fancy-coloured toys. Most will tolerate handling over a period of time. As you have seen from these pages, some of Tony's animals are fantastic when handled. But they are never truly tame. Even the most-handled reptiles will revert to type — or exhibit 'natural' behaviours — under certain situations, such as extreme stress or the presence of food. Almost every reptile keeper has been bitten by their pets from time-to-time.

Fourth — and this is essential — you must operate within the laws of your country, state or territory. In almost every circumstance, it is illegal to take reptiles from the wild. To do the kind of work Tony does, you require a specific licence. And you generally require a licence to keep native reptiles as pets. Now, depending which state or territory you live in, this may require you to meet certain standards of husbandry. There are licensing limits on the number and species of animals you can keep. Higher 'levels' of licence recognise a keeper's experience and allow more challenging species to be kept. This is to prevent first-time keepers from being able to own a Taipan — not an ideal situation. Breeders or retailers of reptiles must also be licensed. You should insist on seeing a sellers' licence before you buy any reptile. And check with your state or territory environment department or agency to get the full details on what is required, before you start planning for that scaly pet.

There are also very strict international quarantine and wildlife laws to prevent the trading in exotic species. You might be living in Australia and really want to keep one of those beautiful African or Asian species you've seen on TV or at the zoo. Or you might be living in another country and have always wanted your own iconic Aussie reptile. Don't be tempted. Exotic reptiles cannot be legally kept in Australia, except under very strict and specific circumstances. Some captive-bred Australian species are available overseas, but check very closely the source of any animals, before you buy. The illegal trade in wildlife continues to thrive and reptiles are a part of that. I worked for the Australian Customs Service for over a decade and I've seen first-hand the cruelty that these smugglers employ. Please, don't support this barbaric trade.

Our final word on keeping reptiles as pets: appreciate the animals you *are* allowed to keep where you live — and keep them well!

Fact Sheet

Stephen's Banded Snake

A small but venomous snake, which is sometimes confused with harmless species.

Identification: Grows to just over 1 metre. Generally black, with white or cream bands. Individuals may be heavily banded or plain.

Diet: Eats lizards, frogs, small birds and mammals. Venomous and potentially dangerous.

Where found: North-east NSW and South-east Queensland, including areas such as the Gold Coast and around Brisbane.

Tony says: These guys vary in colour. They can be banded, with white or darker cream bands, or almost plain. The major difference between this guy and the Bandy Bandy is the Bandy's stripes are bright and uniform. They also have a wider head than a Bandy. Most importantly, these fellows will strike readily if provoked. They are mainly nocturnal, but I do sometimes find them in and around homes. They have a nasty bite and are potentially dangerous, so should not be messed with. If you see one, call an expert.

Stephen's Banded Snake

Chapter 12

Tony's Reptile Show

Mobile show - Tony's demonstrations are full of information.

Are human beings born with an innate — an inborn — fear of snakes and other reptiles? Is it pre-programmed into our DNA? Or is it something we learn as we grow; as people tell us these things are dangerous or bad; as we see how people react when they see a snake? I'm a writer, not an anthropologist, but I suspect both play a part — and it's mostly the latter.

The 'Awareness' part of the name *Reptile Relocation and Awareness* is very important to Tony. His business is not just about snake catching. Tony is passionate about conservation and the role of education in the preservation and protection of wildlife — especially reptiles. He honestly believes that educating the public about the truth of reptiles can make a big difference in the way humans and reptiles interact.

~ ~ ~

Part of the education program involves running kid's parties. As a third-party observer, it's brilliant to watch this tattoo-tough snake wrangler, with his bikie shades and his camo pants, playing 'king of the kids.' There's a beautiful absurdity to the situation, which I can't quite put my finger on. But it doesn't matter. Tony has those kids transfixed!

Watching the faces of young children as they come face-to-face with a new animal is amazing. Their eyes light with wonder. Curiosity. Eagerness. But I don't see fear. That's because they trust Tony. They believe what he tells them. If he says it's OK to touch something, they go ahead and touch. He doesn't want to scare them. He's not carrying on to make a point.

'Here's dear old Mrs Fattbottom,' Tony says, as the kids all crowd around to have a look at his Shingleback. He begins to explain why the lizard's bottom is the same basic size and shape as its head. The kids all want a pat. Some take pictures with their little cameras or phones. A few, now that they've had a pat of Mrs Fatbottom, begin to wonder what else Tony has in his plastic tubs. They're not afraid. They're curious. They want to learn and interact with these animals. I can only hope the experience stays with them — that they aren't tainted in the future by negative information about reptiles.

Tony is very selective about which animals he uses in shows — especially where children are involved. They must have the correct temperament, and even then, at no time does Tony put kids in a situation where they could be bitten or scratched by an animal. Children are allowed to pat and touch his animals, but under very strict and controlled conditions.

'My message is about the preservation and conservation of reptiles. I'm not into scaring people, be they kids or adults, by letting them get bitten. Nor do I make a point of letting animals bite me. I'm not sure that's what it's all about.'

~ ~ ~

Tony has the ability to take his reptile shows on the road. He has an impressive touring set-up which allows him to present his shows across the Gold Coast as well as south-east and central Queensland. He owns an ex-Ambulance, emblazoned with images of snakes and lizards, as well as a custom-built box trailer. This allows him to transport everything he needs, including animals and all his kit. All his vehicles — even his two motorbikes — are mobile billboards for his business — and for reptile education. And he has some other impressive equipment.

Many of Tony's shows are delivered from a magnificent six metre long marquee, which is purpose built for his needs and features the company business signage along with stunning images of his animals. He has a full sound system, lighting, and all the support gear he needs, including first aid equipment. He even has his own folding chairs for patrons, which are set out before the shows. It's an impressive set-up.

Tony's live shows are full of information. These include handling demonstrations of Australia's most venomous snakes. I've seen plenty of snake demonstrators over the years, but watching Tony's 'Top Ten Venomous' show stands out. It really is a great way to spend an hour or so. There's so much to learn.

He steps out onto his stage, a headset microphone in place, which leaves his hands free — a good thing when you're about to handle deadly venomous animals. Over to the side of the display area he has a series of large plastic tubs. Inside a couple of the lighter-coloured tubs are the unmistakeable shapes of moving serpents. The amazing pictures on the walls of the marquee are a taste of what we're about to see.

'How we all doing?' Tony says as the show begins.

His style is easy-going. Authentic. It's not all hyped-up and melodramatic. You feel confident with what he's telling you. He shares his stories and information and you believe him. Trust him. If you had a huge Taipan curled up on the seat of your outside dunny, you feel like this is the bloke you'd want to turn up and help.

He works through his tubs, producing different species of

snake, talking to the audience about their behaviour and dispelling many of the myths we've developed about these creatures over the years. We see the Stephen's Banded Snake and a series of Black Snake species. We see the Death Adder and the King Brown. He shows us a Tiger snake. But, like any good entertainer, Tony leaves his big numbers for the end of the show.

The Coastal Taipan is the third most venomous snake in Australia. An iconic species, with a bad reputation. Naturally, this critter gets one of the final slots in Tony's show.

'These are tough snakes to handle, even for those of us with a lot of experience working with snakes,' Tony says, as he lowers a handling hook and begins to lift the long rusty-coloured snake out of a plastic tub. 'See, I think of snakes like computers. When you want a computer to do something, you press a button or click a link and the computer does it. If you want a snake to react a certain way, you do a certain thing and bingo ... they do it. But these guys aren't like that.'

Right on cue, the Taipan begins trying to slide itself away from the hook Tony has its head resting on. It can't get away, as Tony has a firm, but gentle grip on the tip of the tail. The snake is obviously distracted.

'These guys are a bit smarter.' Tony says. 'They work things out. They don't always react the same way to the same things. One day they will do 'A' and the next they will do 'B'. That means you have to be really careful.'

A couple of people move around at the side of the marquee. The Taipan isn't pleased. It keeps twitching and moving its head around, trying to see what's happening. It's not behaving the way Tony needs it to. He quickly explains about the colouration and behaviour of Australia's largest venomous snake, and then he quickly puts it back into the safety of the tub. No point in risking something terrible, just to be entertaining.

'OK,' Tony says, sliding the Taipan tub away and replacing it with a similar light blue example. 'Time for number two.'

He opens the tub and gently lifts out Isabelle, his 'tame' Eastern Brown Snake. Unlike other Eastern Browns we've met in this book, Isabelle is not the slightest bit twitchy or agitated. Tony puts her down on the floor of the marquee to let her stretch out, while he explains what to do if you see a snake in your back yard. It's the same message as you've found throughout this book: 'leave it alone and call an expert if you are concerned.'

'Ahh, she really is a good girl,' Tony says, as he gently picks Isabelle up again. 'I've owned her now for about seven years. Prior to that she lived down south, being milked for her venom to make antivenene. So it's fair to say, with these shows and all the anti-venom she has helped produce, Isabelle has helped to save a lot of lives.'

It's a nice touch. Here is an Eastern Brown — the species of snake we constantly read about as a killer — being celebrated as a life-saver. That's what I call a positive conservation message.

With Isabelle back in her tub, it's time for number one. Tony slides out a larger plastic tub — this time jet black — for the most venomous land animal on planet earth.

'This species is normally pretty placid,' he says. Then he smiles; 'normally.'

It's great little touch of theatre.

'Now this snake bit its old owner. The owner almost died. So the owner sold him to me. If this snake was a human, I reckon it'd have a name like Charles Manson.'

The audience laughs. A few folk start to minutely shuffle their chairs back from the marquee. They're ready for anything now. Tony gently lifts a huge yellow and black-flecked snake out of the tub. Inland Taipan. Western Taipan. Small-scaled Snake. Fierce Snake. Tony explains about this species' behaviour, shows off the colouration, but all the while I notice he's watching the head of the snake very closely. He's looking for any signs. Watching the animal's behaviour. Understanding and reacting to keep everything safe and calm. In a few minutes, the Fierce Snake is safely back in his tub and Tony uses the opportunity to explain what he would do if the snake was to actually bite him. It's the perfect moment to explain snake bite first aid. A bite, even one involving the most toxic venom on earth, is survivable if you do the right thing. (And if you've forgotten what the right thing is, please got back to page 60 and refresh your memory.)

And then the show is over. Tony hangs around the marquee to answer questions and pose for a photo or two. Then he's off for a break. Rest the voice. Have a cool drink. He has another show this afternoon.

Fact Sheet

Coastal Taipan

This famous — and sometimes infamous — species of snake has a reputation as something to avoid. There's a reason for this.

Identification: Australia's longest venomous snake, the Taipan can grow to a length of over 2.5 metres. They range in colour from olive to dark rusty brown and occasionally darker. They have cream bellies with orange or pink flecks and distinctive pale cream faces.

Diet: Taipans eat only mammals, usually rodents. Larger specimens may tackle small marsupials such as bandicoots.

Where found: Northern Australia, from the Kimberley to north of Brisbane and occasionally further south. Regularly seen around cities such as Cairns and Darwin.

Tony says: While I don't see these guys on the Gold Coast, I have kept them for many years and I can honestly say this is one snake that grabs my attention. Taipans deserve a lot of respect. They are smart — at least by snake standards — and they take notice of everything you do. They also have a very long strike range and the longest fangs of any Australian venomous snake. And while not quite as venomous as their cousin — the Fierce Snake — Taipans still have the third most toxic venom on any land snake on earth. If you live in tropical areas, avoid leaving out food that might attract rats and mice to your land, because this fellow loves eating rodents. And if you do see one of these guys around your place, don't try and deal with it yourself, call an experienced snake handler or wildlife authority.

Coastal Taipan

Chapter 13

Swimming With Crocs

At home with crocs. Tony and Kuzcio the Saltwater Croc.

Just like snakes, crocodiles are an animal which have captivated, fascinated and terrified people for centuries. There are very few opportunities people have to get close to a crocodile — and live to tell the tale. Tony's *Reptile Relocation and Awareness* Croc Adventures allowed people to actually swim with live crocodiles, in a way that was safe for both the animal and the people.

A pool full of gorgeous little crocs. It's not the sort of thing you see too often. It was a great thing to see.

'We used juvenile animals, both Estuarine (Saltwater) and Freshwater species,' Tony says. 'We're accredited by the Australian Wildlife Society to keep crocodiles and we've even had the National Parks bring confiscated pet crocs to stay with us. We keep them until they reach a certain size and then they are returned to croc farms up north. With the Croc Adventures, we would bring along smaller crocodiles to a client's party or event. If the client had access to a swimming pool, we would also allow an opportunity for them to swim with the crocs in a safe and supervised way. The animals had their jaws secured, which was completely harmless to the croc and makes them safe to handle. The pool water is good for the animals as it helps keep their skin healthy and clean. And the events were closely supervised by experienced handlers, so was safe for the clients too. In all the times we ran these events, wehad a perfect safety record. It's a shame we don't run them anymore. Maybe one day we'll do it again.'

'I'm a big believer in conservation through education and excitement,' Tony reminds me. 'We use the events to share some facts and clear up some of the myths about crocodiles. Plus, it's amazing for people to see these animals swimming. You don't normally get the chance to see them in clear water. You know; the beauty of their colours and the effortless way they move. I reckon most went away from those events with a new found love and respect for crocodiles.'

Chapter 14

The Real Deal

Tony and Tiger the Lace Monitor working on the set of Real Doctors

There's a story on the Channel Seven News that catches my attention: a family dog has been bitten by an Eastern Brown Snake on the Gold Coast. The dog was lucky to survive. The reporter wants to speak to the local expert about the prevalence of snakes so early in the season. That reporter speaks to Tony Harrison.

Another day, another news story: a big Carpet Python has eaten two pet guinea pigs and two Gold Coast residents are in hospital after being bitten by snakes. The TV News people want to speak to someone about how we can live alongside snakes. So they call up Tony.

Or this one: there are rumours of crocodiles living in the canals of upmarket Gold Coast suburbs. Tony is approached by the TV reporters for a comment. Outside of a released pet, he thinks it's highly unlikely that there are crocs living as far south as the Gold Coast.

Tony's work has been featured on TV for many years. He's has made numerous appearances on the Sunrise breakfast show. Host Melissa Doyle was certainly impressed with his exploits. During an interview with Tony in 2011, she described him as 'an amazing and tough guy.' Co-host Matthew White just thought he was mad.

Over at the rival Today Show, during an outdoor broadcast on the Gold Coast, host Lisa Wilkinson nursed Shrek, Tony's pet Green Tree Python *(Morelia viridis)*. I remember she described the experience as 'sensual.' Now I assume she meant the working with the snake, not Tony! Co-host Karl Stefanovic kept his distance. 'Snakes are disgusting,' was his verdict.

Then, just to spice things up, entertainment reporter Richard Wilkins came wandering along with someone's pet poodle. 'I brought along breakfast,' he chuckled, holding up the small white fluffy pet.

'I wouldn't put a dog near that snake,' Tony warned, and everyone laughed.

'No, seriously,' Tony replied. 'Not near that one.'

Meanwhile, oblivious to looming canines, Shrek busied himself by burying through one of Ms Wilkinson's elaborate earrings.

'Now that's what I call a fashion accessory,' Tony quipped.

It was too much for Karl. 'I'm outta here,' he chuckled. 'I'm going back to the desk.'

~ ~ ~

Tony does well on TV. His practical, common-sense information comes across well to an audience. As with his live shows, there is an authenticity about him. You get the feeling he's the real deal, even before you see him tackle that Eastern Brown.

He's not into making a big fuss. He's not interested in carrying on — quoting the man himself — 'like a pork chop.' He tells you what's what. He shows you the beauty and wonder of reptiles, and yes, the danger as well.

Totally Wild is a long-running show, primarily aimed at young people, which features stories about youth issues, animals and the environment. Tony has been called the show's 'resident snake expert.' He has presented segments about snakes and his animals have also been used on other stories.

In the landmark 2012 ABC TV series *Great Southern Land*, Professor Steve Simpson wanted to talk about the impact of human habitation as it continued expanding into the natural world. One of the issues he tackled was people moving to the fringes of our largest cities and the challenges of this life 'life on the edge', such as living in close proximity to venomous snakes. In this episode he featured the work of Tony Harrison.

'People would be shocked by the numbers of snakes there are around,' he tells the camera. Then he takes the crew out on a snake call to catch an Eastern Brown in a customers' bathroom.

And it hasn't just been in Australia where Tony has been on TV. He was featured in a story on a German 'science-tainment' TV show called *Galileo*, debunking myths about snake venom. I must say, his German seemed faultless, even if his voice had noticeably changed.

There can be a downside to having a public profile — especially in the reptile 'industry', where unfortunately, not everyone gets along with each other.

'It's a pity,' Tony tells me. 'You know, we should all be working together to promote the preservation and conservation of reptiles. Don't get me wrong, some of us get along really well — a lot of us — but there are others...'

And in these days of social media and instant news, this means the truth can sometimes be an ill-defined thing.

It was early January 2014 — around the time we were finishing the words for this book — and Tony was busy cleaning out cages in his snake room. One of his less-trustworthy pets is a Rough-scaled Snake, an animal which he has owned for some time. This species of snake has a reputation for being a little nervous and prone to bite and Tony's pet is no exception. Tony was in the process of removing the Rough-scale for a cage clean when the snake noticed one of his pet dogs, asleep across the other side of the room.

'My dogs are not allowed near my snakes, for obvious reasons,' Tony explains. 'But the Roughie spotted my little Chihuahua asleep across the room and started heading out of the cage in that direction. I went to steer the snake back in the right direction and it turned around at took a swing at me. Gave me a scare, I can tell you.'

Rough-scale Snakes have potentially dangerous venom. Tony has procedures in place for dealing with such incidents. He immediately applied first aid and within a short time he was admitted to the Gold Coast University Hospital. While he was in hospital, Tony began to experience facial swelling and breathing difficulties. Doctors took blood samples and these were to confirm that he had not, in fact, been injected with any venom by the snake, but had suffered some form of allergic reaction. These types of reactions can be caused by a variety of factors, from traces of venom on the snake's fangs, or from faeces or uric acid (urine) that may have been present on or around the snake's mouth.

'It's not the first time it's happened,' Tony says. 'These 'dry bites' are a warning thing. They are the snake's way of saying; 'watch out pal, next time it will be for real.' But, even though it's not a proper bite, I still have a reaction.'

As a precaution, the hospital kept Tony in overnight for observation. This allowed time for his symptoms to subside, and then he was allowed home. He received no anti-venom treatment. His hospital discharge papers stated he'd suffered anaphylaxis (allergic reaction).

But all hell broke loose.

As events were unfolding, Tony's family and friends began sharing the news via social media. It's what happens in times like these. People were concerned. Upset. I personally received a text message from Tony on the same afternoon as he was admitted to hospital. He told me that he was a bit uncomfortable, but didn't think he'd received any venom in the bite, and he was waiting for the doctors to confirm this through blood tests. He even sent me a picture of himself to show me his swollen 'man boobs.' He was cracking jokes about himself. I knew then he would be OK.

Unfortunately, if good news travels fast, bad news goes at light speed. Social media soon came to life with stories about Tony's situation. A number of people put up posts containing inflammatory and incorrect statements. And someone contacted the media.

Next morning, a local tabloid newspaper on the Gold Coast ran a story alleging 'reckless behaviour' on Tony's part, claiming he had been bitten by a potentially deadly snake and received anti-venom treatment.

'I can only assume a rival operator contacted the paper to report what had happened,' Tony says. 'At least, what they believed happened. I'm not going to waste my time here fencing with other snake handlers, but to be accused of recklessness by someone who did not have all the facts was pretty annoying at the time. It was turned into a personal attack on me.'

The paper concerned was contacted, but refused to retract the story or write a correction. However, a few days later, rival Queensland newspaper ran a story, which gave a much more detailed version of events and this corrected some of the incorrect reports from the earlier publication. One of the local radio stations had Tony on air, which gave him the chance to explain to everyone that he was fine and to further correct the misinformation.

I ask Tony how these things affect him.

'The snake bite was the least of my dramas,' he says, somewhat ironically. 'Look, you take the good with the bad. I've had my head on TV and, that gives you a profile I guess. It makes you a target for some. That's cool. I understand. But to be accused of recklessness is really annoying. I mean, if you believed what some people were saying, I was skylarking around with the Roughie in my backyard, while my dogs roamed wild and next thing you know, I was on death's door in hospital receiving anti-venom. Maybe it would have made a better yarn if that had been the case, but it just wasn't true. Anyway, I'm just happy it was a minor incident, and now I can get back on with my work.'

And there can be an upside to publicity — even when it's adverse. 'Enquiries for my services have actually increased after this incident,' Tony tells me. 'I've had so much support from some really great people. Plus I've had the chance to revisit my procedures and they are all being professionally documented so I can improve the quality of my business even further.'

~ ~ ~

Even if you haven't seen Tony's face on the screen, or read articles in the newspaper, chances are you've seen one or more of his animals. Tony has supplied reptile 'actors' for a wide range of television and movie productions. Tony's reptiles have been used in TV ads, music videos, and in promotional work. If you watched *Big Brother*, *Sea Patrol*, *Reef Doctors*, the Australian version of *Terra Nova*, the movie *Nim's Island,* then you've probably seen some of Tony's scaly performers.

Now, the entertainment industry has a long-held saying: 'never work with children or animals.' I ask what some of the challenges are for Tony, working on TV or movie sets with reptiles.

'Mostly it's the boredom,' Tony grunts. 'It's like nothing happens. You get on set at 6am, sit around for ten hours and contribute to five minutes worth of filming. Thankfully I work with reptiles, and they are happy to chill out in their tubs until they are required and then those intense lights set up for the filming tend to heat them up and away we go. I mean, the experience varies. Some days, I have to tell you, the hours drag by. On some productions you're lucky to get a cup of tea and a biscuit, but on others ... mate ... they put on a four-course spread every meal. Not good for the waistline, but ... you know...'

Tony has plenty of other stories about life on the set.

'One of the funniest was finding out my pet Lace Monitor, Tiger, is just like me — he's scared of heights. Now Lacies are natural tree climbers, but Tiger lives the cosy life at my place. So when he was asked to do a scene in *Reef Doctors*, where he had to climb down a big tree, things kind of went pear-shaped. Tiger and I were lifted high up beside the tree in a cherry picker and I put him on a branch and expected him to slowly climb down as they filmed. But as soon as I looked at him, at his behaviour, I could tell he was freaking out. It was like, "Hey dad, what the hell are you putting me up here for? I'm really not enjoying this." The film crew got their shots in the end, but not before I insisted on them stretching out a safety net to catch Tiger if he fell.'

A safety net for a Lace Monitor! OK, I think I've heard it all now.

There's another famous scene involving Tony's reptiles, this time from the show *Sea Patrol*.

'In the script there was an incident with a reptile smuggler and they needed a whole heap of snakes to crawl around on camera. So we used 27 of my pythons; little Children's and Stimson's, some bigger ones like Olives and Carpets. I tipped over their tubs from off camera and let them slide out at their own speed — and into the shot. It worked out great.'

Sounds easy enough so far. And I actually remember watching that episode of the show. I remember there was a scene with a Brown snake. I ask Tony if that was one of his critters?

'Yeah, it was. Or should I say "they" were. The directors wanted a venomous snake in a scene. The trouble was; they wanted a 'tame' snake that would also arc up and become angry on cue. You know, like a trained seal. Like that type of snake exists! Luckily for them, I have my two Eastern Browns — (Not Happy) Jan and Isabelle — who look pretty much the same, but have very different temperaments. Isabelle is a pussy cat, and she lay there nice and calmly for the shots with the actors at a safe distance. Then, for the close up stuff, they put the actors behind a thin Perspex screen while I replaced Isabelle with Jan. I was dressed in navy clobber, just at the edge of the shot and I went "boo" and waved my arms around, and Jan carried on like a champion. The directors were stoked, it was a great scene.'

Sometimes things just work out, even without Tony's intervention.

'We're working on a new production at the moment,' Tony tells me. 'It's called *Skin*. In one particular scene, they wanted footage of a Carpet Python shedding. Now snakes don't shed on cue, and none of my animals were in shed at the time of the shoot. Anyway, someone from the show found a freshly-shed Carpet Python skin and they lay it out on a branch. Then we put my big old Carpet, Diesel, onto the branch and hoped he would move along the skin, like it was his shed. Problem is, the shed was from a female Carpet, and Diesel is a male. He started tasting that shed with his tongue and he went nuts. It was like, "Oh yes, they've given me a girlfriend!" He was all over that shed, searching for the female snake that had to be inside somewhere. I thought we were stuffed — that the shoot would be a disaster. But then, as the cameras rolled, Diesel stuck his head inside the head of the shed skin and then pushed out of it, just like he was actually shedding himself. It was spot-on!'

~ ~ ~

When he's not coercing his animals to perform for someone else's camera, Tony is taking shots of his own. With a few exceptions, all the stunning photographs you see in this book were taken by Tony himself. Photography is one media where he can combine his love of reptiles with another of his passions. He's been fortunate enough to work with some of the great photographers; people like Shannon Plummer and Steve Parish. Under his house, down where most of his critters live, Tony has an impressive set up for taking his images.

'This actual unit here came from the film *Terra Nova*,' Tony explains.

It's a great little set: an open enclosure on a stand, and on caster wheels, to allow it to be moved around. Around the perimeter of the stand is a Perspex shield, which allows for close-up and macro shots of even the most venomous subject.

'I can easily change the furniture in the set to suit the species,' Tony says. 'If I'm shooting a rainforest frog, it doesn't look right on orange sand. So I put in some greenery and away we go. This set gives me the flexibility to change things around and enhance the image. I shoot against a black background, with lights for illuminating the set as well as lights designed to enhance the colours of the animal being photographed.'

Yet, the technology is only part of the equation. Having the trick gear is important, and there are plenty of great animal images out there, but it's Tony's knowledge of his subjects that makes his shots so powerful. If he wants to capture a particular 'look' or pose, he knows how to cooperate with the animal to achieve that pose.

'For example, if I want to get an image of a snake showing its fangs, I need to get an open-mouthed shot,' he explains. 'The easiest way to do this is to feed the animal in the set and then be ready. Most snakes will 'yawn' after a meal, to help bring their jaw muscles back into alignment. This is when I get the shot. It's great in theory, but it doesn't always work in practice.'

Like any subject, reptiles can be difficult or easy subjects. Some are just natural-born performers.

'And some are just nightmares,' Tony adds. 'You want them to face left, they'll face right. You want them to stand up, they'll lie down. Sometimes you just have to admit defeat and try again later, or use another animal. Some though … I remember a wild Rough-scaled Snake I caught a little while back. I had to hold him overnight before he was released, so I used the opportunity to get some pictures of him. Talk about a poser! I just had to put this guy down, focus the camera and away he'd go. He puffed himself up, stood there and posed perfectly. He stuck out his tongue, he flattened out his head, mate he did everything I wanted. All I had to do was focus in and start firing off shots. Check out the Fact Sheet for Rough-scaled Snakes, we used one of those shots there. Awesome.'

~ ~ ~

Photography is just one media Tony is using to spread his message about the conservation of reptiles. And, as we've seen, he has many others. You've read some of his stories in these pages. You had a glimpse into the life of a snake catcher and reptile expert. Hopefully you've learned a few facts, and we've dispelled a few myths. Maybe you will be better equipped to deal with the next snake or other reptile you come across in your travels. If that's the case, then this project will have been worthwhile.

In any case, I thought it was appropriate for Tony to have the final word. And, just as I was thinking this, he gave me a call.

Fact Sheet

Rough-scaled Snake

This is a dangerously venomous snake species which, unfortunately, looks very similar to the harmless Keelback.

Identification: Grow to about 1 metre in length. They have slightly keeled or rough scales and vary in colour from army green to brown to gun-metal grey. They may have black dots, flecks or bands on their bodies.

Diet: Eats frogs and lizards, as well as small mammals and even birds. This species is venomous and potentially dangerous to humans.

Where found: Two main localities — Northern NSW to the Fraser Coast of Queensland and also in the Wet Tropics of Far North Queensland. Found around Brisbane, the Gold Coast and near Cairns.

Tony says: I always think this is a snake that was wired wrongly. What I mean by that is these guys are really defensive and will strike repeatedly at a predator, no matter how big that predator is. Unfortunately, these guys also look quite a lot like a Keelback, which is a harmless species that does us all a favour by helping to eliminate the Cane Toad. Both species eat frogs and both have a preference for moist areas. I have seen so many instances where Keelbacks have been killed thinking they were these guys. Roughies can also look a little like Eastern Brown or Tiger Snakes, depending on their colouration. And, as we've discovered, the colour of a snake seldom determines the species. While I don't see a lot of these snakes, they are around and people should leave them alone. If you see one and are not sure if it's a harmless Keelback or one of these guys, my recommendation is to stay clear and call an expert to assist if you are concerned.

Rough-scaled Snake

A Night with Tony

Tony inside Tiger.

It's a couple of weeks before Christmas, 2013. A busy time. My days are filled with attempts to meet pre-holiday deadlines; before nights of barbeques and parties. I'm tired. I decide to take a few minutes out for myself, sitting quietly in the semi-dark as light rain whispers on the roof of our house. After 18 hours of screaming, the cicadas have finally fallen silent. The sky is the colour of raw sapphire.

A metre from where I sit, my pet python begins gliding across his enclosure, his tongue dancing, his head and neck climbing the glass, eager to see whether I bring the promise of a meal. I don't, but he moves himself into a good position, just in case I change my mind. I look at his delicate brown and cream face; each scale perfectly aligned with its neighbour; shiny brown cat's eyes; the heat pits along his jaw; the way his skin has a rainbow shimmer in the light. He is not some demonic creature, bent on my destruction. And neither are his wild relatives.

I remember back to those childhood days, watching Harry Butler on TV. He always had a sentiment. It used to resonate with me then and it still does today. He believed humans had to find ways to coexist with animals. Our cities, our industry, our influence, are all expanding out into the natural world. That growth isn't going to stop. This means human beings and animals will need to increasingly find ways to live together. And the effort will need to come from our side of the ledger. Because when human and natural worlds collide — it's overwhelmingly the animals who suffer.

These are the things I'm thinking as my mobile phone rings. It's getting late. I'd hoped to have finished work for the day, indeed for the week, but now ... Anyway, I take the call, it could be a client. It could be important.

It is important. It's Tony Harrison.

'How you going Mister Writer?' he asks.

'Good mate. So, you still working at this hour?' I say, knowing full well he would be.

'Yep, I'm out and about. Getting ready to catch a Keelback. Listen, I just wanted to let you know I've read through the final manuscript and I thought I'd ring to say it's exactly what I envisaged when we started out on this project. You have no idea how many people ask me the same questions day in and day out. And I keep answering them, because most books or TV shows about reptiles don't cover the things most everyday people want to know. They give you a photo or they tell you about the natural history of a snake or whatever. You know; they look at what it hunts or what hunts it. Biology stuff. I wanted this book to tell people the sorts of things to do if they see a snake or other reptile in their own backyards. What to look out for. The kind of critters they are actually likely to see. Ways to help keep themselves safe. You know; all that good practical stuff. Now we have this, it's like I have a permanent way to get the message out there.'

'That's excellent,' I reply. 'As we've been progressing, so many people have asked me what the book is about, and when I've told them, they are really interested — even if they aren't into reptiles.'

'Yeah, exactly. It's why I started out in this business, you know, raising awareness about reptiles and hoping to save a few animals from being needlessly killed. And now ... well, here we are.'

We chat for a few more minutes and then Tony has to go

to catch his latest snake. It's another one of those animals he was just speaking of — an animal at risk of being killed for no other reason than what it is. One of the good guys labelled bad — by humans.

~ ~ ~

It really is about time we took a reality check when it comes to reptiles — especially snakes. Unless you're someone like Tony Harrison, coming face-to-face with a deadly serpent is unlikely to be the most dangerous thing you will do today. Or tomorrow. Or ever. According to the Australian Road Deaths Database — more than 1300 people killed were on Australian roads in 2012.[1] This compares to a handful of folk who die each year due to snake bite. And while even a single death is tragic, were the fear and loathing many people have for snakes to be transferred to the motor car, Australian roads would be very quiet places indeed.

In this book Tony and I have tried to enlighten you, through providing information, but also some entertainment. Through words and pictures. Through facts, not fallacies. It's what Tony Harrison has been trying to do for almost 20 years. And I strongly suspect it's what he'll continue to do for at least 20 more.

---

1 www.bitre.gov.au/statistics/safety/fatal_road_crash_database.aspx

Reptile Resources

Reptile Relocation and Awareness website:
http://www.goldcoastsnakecatcher.com.au/

Tony's Phone number: 0401 263 296.

Tony's YouTube Channel:
www.youtube.com/channel/UCaTFJoogQOxxcben7MZxkEQ

Other websites with information relevant to the protection and keeping of native reptiles include:

QLD Department of Environment and Heritage Wildlife Portal:
www.ehp.qld.gov.au/wildlife/

NSW Department of Environment:
www.environment.nsw.gov.au/

Victorian Department of Environment and Primary Industries:
www.dse.vic.gov.au/

WA Department of Environment and Conservation:
www.dec.wa.gov.au/

SA Department of Environment:
www.environment.sa.gov.au/Home

NT Department of Land and Resource Management:
lrm.nt.gov.au/

ACT Directorate of Environment:
www.environment.act.gov.au/

Correct as at 01 March 2014

.

www.ingramcontent.com/pod-product-compliance
Lightning Source LLC
Chambersburg PA
CBHW050842270326
41930CB00019B/3435